Ab Antiquo, Ab Aeterno

A Collection of Poetry and Prose

by

Brandon Gene Petit

Copyright © 2010 Brandon Gene Petit. All Rights Reserved.

No part of this book may be reproduced or transmitted by any means without the written permission of the author.

Published by Orchestrion – Port Jervis, New York   2010

ISBN-13:   978-0-615-38233-3

LCCN: 2010909135

In loving memory of

Madison & Nathan Baxley

May you enjoy your home beyond home

You can tell reality apart from dream,

But you can't tell dream apart from reality...

Contents

Dream Logue One	1
The Cosmic Drifter	3
Worlds Remembered	4
Where Myth Never Dies	5
A Fool's Lament	6
The Utopist	7
Not the One	8
Catharsis	9
To Speak of Nicole	10
The Ogre and the Diamond	11
Paramnesia	12
Without Flesh, Without Fear	13
Memoriter	14
Sidereal Lover	15
Noctiphilia	16
To the Perfect Enemy	17
Trespassers' Union	18
Prelude to Lilith	19
Dark Hours	20
He Who Remains	21
Welcome One	22
Fuel for a Forgotten Tale	24
The Mercy Seekers	26

Show You	27
Out There	28
Behold	29
Strange Nights	30
She Awaits	31
The Right Shade of Pain	32
Solitaire	34
Contemptuous	35
Fluke	36
The Portal is Open	37
Heathen Moon	38
In Her Absence	40
A War between Wizards	41
The Valley of Virgo	42
Dunning Lake	43
Layers of Me	44
Glimpsing the Demon	45
To a Girl with Green Eyes	46
The Wiccan Dove	47
Lorn	48
An Angel in Question	50
Dream Logue Two	51
In Debt to Love	52
Dear Aesthete	53
Molding the Hero	54

Into the Oils	56
Women Astray	57
Romance of the Winds	58
A Study in Sorrow	59
The Insomniac in Love	60
Laburnine Lullaby	61
Wayward Spirits	62
Against the Word	64
A Curse Upon You	65
View from a Coward's Den	66
She is Legend	67
Home Beyond Home	68
I'll Forget You Yet	69
The Lost Art of Sanity	70
Hermit's Eden	72
Sympathy for the Abyss	73
Fallen (Into Place)	74
Two Rivers	75
Matters of Time and God	76
In Another Life	77
Beauty in Brown	78
Striking a Nerve	79
Then and Only Then	80
The Waiting of the Widow	81
Nescience	82

Sentimental Circles	83
The Wolves of Bathroe	85
Mare Clausum	86
Court of Eons Passed	87
Needless to Say	89
Clear My Conscience	90
So it is Written	91
The Storm Herald	92
You Are Joy	94
Lentissimo	95
In Weeping for Lost Bibelots	96
The Hole	98
Autumn in Babylon	99
I Among Others	100
Canaan	101
Heir to Enigma	102
A Thousand Ways	103
Amygdala	104
Mirror Envy	106
Invert Your Oars	107
Tributaries	108
A Pledge to Xenia	109
Looking Back, I Love Her	111
Something of a Gem	112
A Delayed Affair	113

Favor the Strong	114
Seldom	115
The Goodhill Manor	116
Under Lights, Over Wine	118
All Walks of Life	119
London Sleeps Not Tonight	120
In Low Light	122
Observe and Obey	123
Neglecting Oblivion	125
She Poses with Spiders	126
Banished	127
Her Majesty to Wed	128
Hearts without Quarrel	129
Midnight Meanings	130
Auras in Bloom	131
Travelers Beware	132
A Rebirth of Chances	133
If You So Choose	134
Hemlock Street	135
The Greatest of Powers	137
On His Watch	138
I Am in Awe	139
Heaven's Circuit	140
'Tis a Journey	141
Words, Merely Words	142

Dream Logue One

When sleep finally arrives, a window opens inside the dull room that is my waking mind and my soul scrambles out from the watch of a sedated guard. Out into a forbidden moonlit garden leaps everything but my flesh, each night dwelling deeper into an inner realm through a series of meaningless quests. Clouded yet stunning images expand into an eternal weave, and forgotten thoughts crawl out from the darkest far corners of my brain. Nameless emotions pulse, tingle, and ripple through the hole where physical laws once clustered, as an intensely populated infinity beckons to me from where a twilight sun glowers sentiently.

With heavy heart and hungry eyes I follow my instincts through a parallel universe where drunken acts of the mind play the role of gods, fumbling about in a vivid yet virtually noiseless world where my most obscure fears and spiritual desires collapse and reform in endless polypous waves. Landscapes lush in detail spill from the pages of cherished childhood literature, cleverly concealing the curious residents read of in text. Dimly painted forests and oddly sketched towns drip with intimidation as well as curiosity, while a mother's bittersweet comfort pervades the air despite not a single human being in sight.

Houses are museums littered with enigmatic objects, castles whose innermost chambers are explored only by bold, night-roaming felines. A flight of densely carpeted stairs leads to an endless hallway lined with half-opened doors, attached to rooms mostly empty and dark. Mirrors old and new encase portraits of my alter egos, lit by tiny flames that twitch on the tips of various tabletop candles. Back doors lead to forests of deceptive size, divided by serpentine walkways and teetering wooden bridges. An exotic horned mammal drinks from a sparkling fountain, while fish of unusual size flash their quasi-oriental scales in contrast to the murky creeks below.

Outlandish shades of pink, red and lavender burn slowly in an alien sunset, reflecting off the waves of a vast prehistoric sea in a dizzying array of patterns. Strange creatures of flight guard their nests along the shoreline, far from the reach of titanic forms that lurk blindly among the depths where a dense fog hides a rare visit to the surface. Soon stars begin to appear as watched from lonely rooftops, clinging affectionately to a crude spiral that twists forever upward into the deep cerulean void. Shadows and shapes sometimes pass over the moon, scurrying in a rush to re-cloak themselves among the cluttered cosmos. Manifestations of my darker side play in doors and hallways in the form of mischievous poltergeists, toying with doorknobs and light switches or trickling through intricate scenes of urban decay.

The perfect features of childhood loves appear to bleed the senses and then fade again, as fleeting in form as benign ghosts inclined to leave a scented afterglow. A temporary salvation radiates from their candied eyes, causing a comforting tinge of pain to throb where my chest would be in waking life, as the smell of their hair and skin pulls me like a beggar toward a confectionery mirage. Their song comes to me from great distances like the smell of rain across a web of enchanted fields, where golden beads of dew drip like honey from the strings of an angel's harp and elder structures aged like the finest wine tremble to the tune of the thunder god's ire…

The Cosmic Drifter

    I crept out to see the outside on odd nights, when the eye-like stars grew too sleepy to hold their gaze and guard their lonely secrets. I've scampered across forbidden lines like an undetected scavenger, flitting through cracks in time and swimming beneath material space; seeing dreams before they are dreamt, as well as thoughts that are not wholly thoughts. I've beheld untold realms, conceived in the hands of a creator even more furtive and abstracted than our own... realms where pleasure and pain mingle freely, openly exchanging kisses without boundaries between their lips. Here have I seen shapes of infinite chaotic beauty, molded from a primal gel unlike the one our lives had sprung from. Before my dazzled eyes they twisted, bubbled, and broke off into impossible designs that simply couldn't be. My mind endured countless emotions as I hurtled through rich tapestries of vision, bizarre pseudo-realities that defied all semblances of any known heaven or hell. I saw this was the raw thread of nature, before the limbs of order sculpted it into being... the inconceivable underbelly of all existence.

Worlds Remembered

Memories nest in the tracks that time leaves, providing refuge for those that find their daily lives acerbic yet need not the reckless wonders of the cold, unfeeling gulfs. These are the ones who choose to stay behind as time rages on like a blind and fearless juggernaut, making their home the inner spheres where intimate sights and sounds hold sway. Here clouds crawl at a lethargic pace, shielding the cosmic secrets from such timid and untried eyes; allowing only the perfect shade of light to fall on sinless shingled roofs and thickly scented lawns, where streets nearly emptied by a world preoccupied with sleep hum with a strange cicada lullaby. A warm evening breeze snakes through the diorama, creeping in through back screen doors to battle with the gusts thrown from living room fans. Inside familiar smells cling to musty, yellowed walls and the crackle of a man fumbling through a newspaper speckles the otherwise dreary household air. A stained-glass ornament filters cryptic flavors of light onto a cold kitchen floor, while a warm stove window reveals a pie soaking in an amber luminescence. The near subliminal pulse of a dishwasher burrows into the mind of a sleeping child, mimicking a cadence suggested in the womb, and the bold ticks of a clock find their way across a silent room in an effort to invoke a genuine trance.

The gears of a tiny universe labor incessantly, guided by an ambient life force found just within our reach; boasting of innocence unaltered by the outside world and safe from nameless, clawing forces lurking just beyond the rim. Like a world-worn yet devoted lover truthful till the dawn of death, memorabilia safely guarded lingers behind all we see... waiting for some lucky soul to turn a stone and crack its code, whisked away to quiet havens cosseted between our lives.

Where Myth Never Dies

I am told by the most wayward of my forefathers that magic still lingers in hazier parts of the globe, left to pulse in narrow grooves where an erratic age has dried up and left a few shallow pools. Forms pleasant to the eye are still rumored to grow where the roots of cold metal cities have not tainted the soil and invitingly animated springs have touched only the lips of untamed forest familiars... Where the farthest arms of the river thin into sparkling streams that run like veins through an enchanted woodland mass, babbling to an eerie luminescence that gleams with the occasional flailing wisp of detached spider web. A fragrant omnipresence reigns where the small bodies of birds dart in and out of tangled underbrush, and a wizard's wand finds its beginnings in a youthful tree's meandering fingers. Here the songs of sinners do not carry past the nourished leaves, where the trunks of trees bear strange marks uncommon to the urbane man... No, here is only the flutter of elusive wings and the gargling of crystalline waters, where spinning leaves catch a moment of illumination from golden beams of light as they tumble to the forest floor.

Stealth and secrecy are the trends shared by all residing elements, for to shine a lantern into the depths would be to disturb an archaic purity nonadhesive to the wildest bard. I avow not to poison such a paradise with my trampling footsteps, leaving it to flicker at the end of some convoluted fairy route; my sole reason for not seeking out such venerable wonders in their natural state, in far removed places scoffed at by storytellers and ignored by the daily paths of men. I have interviewed this sacred stretch of earth only by sampling its scent on the far-traveled breeze, for my eyes will not bear the guilt of witnessing what was not made for my eyes to see. Only through a painter's oily potions will this secluded universe breathe the same air as I, for the full potency would make the most succulent rainforests and shiniest seas wither like a desert in comparison.

No sword may slash the hindering foliage that serves as a gateway to vistas unframed; no torch may pass but a few timid steps past the first wall of trees into this celibate hollow. Time is not the ruler here, nor is speech nor music nor anything else of modified beauty. Objects of wood are blessed with the endurance of steel, an ironic answer to civilization that remains a monolith to folklore and phantasm. As a mortal I am restricted to milder inventions; I belong only miles from the place of my birth. Besides, who am I to unravel such gifts not intended to please any bipedal being, and leave my mark next to ageless enigmas when I have not lived but a handful of years? Only in my thoughts will I venture that far, past concrete creations that crumble with epochs... My intentions are mild yet nature resists, and my stunted escapades merely circle back home.

A Fool's Lament

     Anguish plays a leading role in the convoluted dance of life, from our first moments in the light upon exiting the womb to our first encounters with the fickleness of love. I, myself, have dabbled in the agony of jealousy, the audacity of shame, and the endurance of guilt… and have come to befriend such compelling demons with a futile unwillingness that surrenders with a muffled sigh. Robbed of all but the simplest pleasures, I fester in my crowded quarters and write of utopias that my eyes may never meet; spacious chimeras lost to the irony of poetic license and fed to the dreaming depths where they belong. Instead I awake to rain-soaked streets and clumps of simple structures, a wintry domain that would be just as glamorous had it not been poisoned with my most recent sorrow. Every sunrise is encoded with the endless plight of wanting and not having, and the ground is marred by the footprints of wonders that came and passed in the night. I watch from my window and wait for their return, my breath painting hot clouds of desperation against frigid gray glass, gripping in my hand flowers meant for a lover that doesn't exist outside my childish musing.

     Contradictions of pride and faith linger in a cloud above my head as I join the sickly circus of misfit fools and weeping clowns, characters all too familiar from a persuasive past. Nature shows its cruelest colors in a world embittered with solid objects, sending back the love I have to give with a bland and faceless cynicism. I gain approval only from the eyes of the smallest child, who judges me not by my deeds but reveres my soul with the gift of receptive wonder. Others accuse me of weakness and shine light on the gifts that lay untouched at my feet, yet I assure them more potent tragedies wait beyond every corner to diversify my palette of pain. So I place the final touches on a brutal self-portrait that no amount of rain can ever melt away, allowing myself to fall into its faded smile and hard lines where the absence of religion has etched an early trace of calloused wisdom… For my travels outside the realms of happiness have taught me much despite my groans, and gloom is an intrinsic element that serves as well as my heart or brain. I see the dawn the same way as those that have renounced their faith, and answer only to the storms that grumble with a mutual rage.

The Utopist

Though I've felt the cream of winter dreams
When the sun-scorched day is through
My fingers wet is all I get
And a glimpse of déjà vu

What a tragic waste, this aftertaste
Gone away like morning dew
But the pieces fit when the moon is lit
And the stars are more than few

A sly Earth sighs under twilight eyes
Yielding wonders false and true
Secrets took with the passing brook
In a chilled ambrosial stew

The spring is long and it'd seem quite wrong
If the skies were forever blue
Let the moonlight flow through the midnight snow
And the flora dim its hue

Let the cold air sting as a church bell rings
And a sleeping world comes to
While a brand new sway to the roles we play
Makes inspiring tales ensue

My cluttered head hasn't been misread
And my heart knows what to do
I explore my range for a graceful change
As I wander roads anew

Not the One

    Luck and chance had brought you to me, but beautiful things come with careful instructions… I've strengthened my years but my roots are in cowardice; a weight on my shoulders will not carry for long. I thrive as a lover but strain as a provider, for the gifts I have to offer are intangible and fleeting. I am but a simplistic magician, trained to deceive you as well as myself. My illusions make you smile but they are sand in the wind, mere tricks upon your eyes kept in limited supply… waning in time they'll soon fail to impress; a dove from my cloak will not shelter our heads. Each day is a wish to transcend modern fairy tales, blatant reality prepping my grave… longing for the day when I take from the top shelf and earn your respect and your hand as a bride. But I cannot make your life swallow smoothly; the bitterest pill that cuts through my slight taste… Our lesions will heal but our paths will divide and they'll rescue you while I descend to the bottom. Maybe a better life waits down the road, perhaps in another pocket of time… where we bury our toes into paradise sands and a kind ocean breeze masks the stench of past troubles. But that world is concealed in an overplayed song that waits deep in my heart as I beg before kings, selling myself while my goals become stagnant for today is not the day and I am not the one.

Catharsis

    I am alive only for those rare moments of authentic euphoria, when a godly peace travels from the farthest horizon to aid me with a sweet inoculation. Tense shivers of anxiety settle into soothing, coherent waves of melancholy, falling in step with a mental metronome that lures me down a stairwell attached to the purest, most uncontaminated slumber. At last enduring fears relax their grip on my psyche, withdrawing into darkness like a vanquished beast retreating into a cave, and an innocent ballad finds its way through the fading dissonance in an effort to restore sanity and order. The angel of mercy descends on me, scattering the vultures that covet the last breaths of my corpse… gathering my pieces up into her wings and cradling me to the rhythm of her unconditional heartbeat. With her comes painterly suggestions of a glorious swan-filled heaven, and the comfort of knowing that loved ones are safely sealed in their respective realms makes surrender an easy task. War-heated blood turns to clean summer rain, and the fiery eyes of foes turn into radiant winter stars. My mistake to drink from a river of venom comes to the end of its reign, as the cool touch of grace massages it from my veins and an enchantress's kiss awakens me to the shores of a world reborn.

    Exhausted from wrestling with the serpent's heavy coils, I allow myself to melt into breathable waters like a crumbling post-winter lake, finally one with the life-giving juices that fatten the roots of an unblemished countryside… where equine forms graze uninterrupted upon plush fields of imperishable green, dotting verdant hills carpeted by strains of untouched wildflower and incensed by disheveled pollens strange to newly embellished senses. Vaguely prismatic skies shimmer with distant sheets of rain, sedating me with ocular pleasures obstructed only by subtle tears of joy… tainted by plumes of ambiguous colors any painter would chase into night-curtained halcyon shades. This is the closest I'll get to caressing the face of divinity, the deepest glimpse I'll ever extract from a crystal ball clouded on more resentful days… but I return from the motherly fire with enough flame to light my current path, gently lifted out of the womblike security of eons encircling and laid into my morning bed. I can still hear the blissful chimes of eternity encrypted among my daily surroundings, whispering promises of future flights that will guide me off that final pier; coaxing me across the remaining chapters of my life where a friendly voice waits with a phrase that will unclench my trembling fist once and for all.

To Speak of Nicole

Never to be purged from my imagination's lonely 'scape
Inimical to hearts of men that grovel in her shadow's drape
Corruption she has tasted but she won't fall far from innocence
Out of sorrow's ashes births the phoenix in magnificence
Living in my memory, she plays her silk symbolic part
Eleven steps ahead of me, she's stronger than the broken heart

Saint-like is the power that she uses to outlive desire
Craving drives a man to madness, never ceases to inspire
Heaven can't describe the longing driven by her lingering vision
Underneath her fragrant smile, the opulence of indecision
Leaning toward her scented aura, redolence for which I yearn
The bloodline of her memory will lead me down where candles burn
Zealous for her perfect poison evident within her lair

…I resurrect a bond in blood reflected in her crimson hair

The Ogre and the Diamond

  Beauty brings pain to those who do not hold it on a leash, and with that pain the tower of pride begins to tumble stone by stone. For what incited hand does not reach for something beautiful, whether that hand be warm and fair or cold and hideously cracked? Even the most defiant ugliness will kneel to the hosts of heaven's scent, peering out from the depths of blasphemy to spy a worthy future queen. Man and beast share mutual anguish, side by side in the universal quest for a prize beyond any reasonable birth right. The race to cage the songbird is on, the age-old sport of pursuing what is not to be contained for long. Just as any prudent man is quick to put his mark on his maiden, to own something precious is to shield it from jealous eyes and withdraw trust in those who are plagued with similar needs and desires. Any unique treasure is tagged with the sleepless duties of paying off its debt and monitoring its attraction to others, but there are those who are willingly diced by the thorns of their favorite rose. Only the empty handed fool dares to question the rules of beauty's game, his disposable tears lost to the soil of an unforgiving kingdom... banished to the wicked wilderness where the ogre demotes his love to a shattered reflection and buries his mind in less desirable tasks.

  But alas, the whole tragic affair is but a daydream in the mind of a restless universe... for the ogre, the fool, and eventually the incurious maiden will fade away into the shifting landscape as casualties of the infinitely layered seasons. Whether this is justice, consolation or just plain irony is up to the perceiver and the resilience of his heart, for even one who has captured beauty must learn to lose it and embrace an even greater truth. But beauty will return in other incarnations, each as fleeting as the last but contributive to an ultimate survival as another pitiless extension of nature... armed with the cruel placidity of indifference and the power to end an unaesthetic drought. The miniature atrocities of love will never completely pull their stingers out of the pelt of consciousness, tainting the blood with a steely curse that will forever transact through humanity's heart... and the tale that tells it all will be immortalized in cliché to entertain those who regard life with awe.

Paramnesia

I have listened to elusive shreds of strange wisdom, and strayed too far from my door on questionable spiritual journeys. I have been dizzied by the fumes of such ego-tickling adrenaline concoctions, only to find myself a pawn in the mind's web of cruel tricks… sitting upright in reality's prison bed with nothing to show for my exhaustive adventures, the spots before my eyes still fresh from the flashing cameras. With not a single witness to cement the gaps in my tale, I must turn and face the undeniable question… Has every working gear in this elaborate spectacle been the stuff of madness? I still wrestle with the illusion everyday, its cobwebbed corners encasing my brain while your head bubbles with numbers and figures… my toes still pointed halfway towards an impossible destiny, unsure to cross the waters I had so confidently walked upon before. No reassuring hand greets my reach into the depths of imagination, and I am left with no choice but to remove the baited hook from my mouth and allow my eyes to dilate to that familiar reasoning light.

But had I not wrestled with foes now banished for their fantastical crimes, and walked with characters that seem to have no place in the present time? Had this vivid display not at least been made from the same flesh as my waking life, twisted into some intangible form to ease potential for mass hysteria? It's true, lessons have been learned and villains have been exiled, but with them many of my most pleasant memories have been vaporized by an earthbound amnesia. This is my punishment for trespassing on phantasmal terrain, a mild but enduring sentence that pervades the last of my days in a now uneventful world… leaving the future an open wound that taunts my subjugated faith and mutes the tales of whispering winds that now have no more tales to tell.

Without Flesh, Without Fear

      I have a name left to me by a world that has long exceeded its final dying sighs... A name that sounds like harsh winter breath in extravagant clouds... A name synonymous with the sentient gleam in a wolf's fathomless eye and as long as all the nights of the Earth connected on one illustrious strand... A name not entirely forgotten, but reserved for a form that will outrun my mortal limbs and thrive in the ebony spaces as a citizen of the wild. No longer weighted by childish fears, I will unlock a primeval love affair between the oldest parts of my soul and the voiceless depths of night, gaining the immunities needed to parallel the forces of nature. My eyes will no longer be blind to miles of nocturnal beauty, and my mind will not shrink from inane superstitions. My skin will no longer flinch under frigid drops of rain, and my bare feet will not dither over rough blades of grass. Under a bleached moon I will haunt the lonely roads that you pass only swiftly in the shell of an automobile or dream about from the safety of your bedroom window, my senses carving a path through the chilled mists that perspire from the woodland voids. I will cross the ebon fields with a swiftness never fueled by fear, transcending every fence and ditch with or without the comfort of a lunar phosphorescence... all to the pulse of an insect choir that chants my esoteric name.

      A brother to the phantoms that sidestep humanity, I will become one with the whispered fables enthroned by a shamanic mystique... forgetful of your sight as I roam the birthplace of so many unshaped nightmares. An aching migratory fever calls to me like the distant sighs of a pan-flute gently unfurling, and my conscience will lead me there as my sole master since it whispered to me in my mother's womb. Bound only to the land that feeds me and the streams that bathe me, I will greet every season's passing with a triumphant cry of survival... never breaking union with the silent instincts that ensure the confidence of my steps. No lover will ever weigh upon my heart, and no grave will ever hold me in its arms. The complex aromas of the Earth will have new riddles for me, replacing the secular dilemmas that have so cleverly distracted me from the natural world's naked splendor, and the trite moments of daylight that enslave you will bring me dreams in a restful hibernation.

      Blessed is the ancient force that moves the slab of its tomb aside and tracks my scent through insufferable eons, rummaging through a cluttered civilization to find me and lure me out of my cowardly niche with a language that I ache to learn. Even now that force converses with my heart in a telepathic fashion, stroking the spine of my inner beast in wait for my final dusk to draw near. Until then each dose of night air weakens the walls of my smothering cocoon, slowly unwinding my mortal fabric to welcome the raw vim of nature into circulation... exposing long idled spiritual viscera to an atmosphere that has bathed my most sanguine ancestors. Soon the bestial vehicle that defies the arrow of evolution will be set in motion, crowning me prince of the unlit paths that weave outside the rigid walls of man and dip into the dark well-waters of eternity... damning the burdens of humanhood to fade with the old name that has narrowed the range of my spirit for too long.

Memoriter

When death liberates me unto its acre
Will I miss the familiar haunts of rejection?
When I'm forced to gaze into the eyes of my maker
Will I miss the sincerity of my reflection?

When my place in the world has withdrawn its intention
Will I long for the tartness of love's pungent lime?
When I find out that death is a wondrous invention
Will I drop all my cares for eternity's climb?

When the reaper reveals to me intricate wonders
Will I miss the warm breeze and the dullness of day?
When my eyes go to shut out humanity's blunders
Will I miss the glad fools that enlightened my stay?

When I glimpse of the laughter that waits beyond doom
Will I still hear the pain in my mother's good-bye?
When letters are chiseling into my tomb
Will I know life again in a new infant's cry?

When a sip from the Lethe dulls my lifelong affections
Will I forget the snow on the tip of my tongue?
When I no longer hunger for earthly confections
Will I still need the one that I fought to become?

Transcending the threshold requires contortion
So desperately wed to the flaws in my form
I bask in the comfort of natural distortion
Can I nourish without the emotional storm?

The talent to bleed, perceive and perspire
Can only be bred in a heart-heavy chest
Will I don a new robe or still wean from desire
When it comes time to lay my old playthings to rest?

Sidereal Lover

Sometimes I fancy that our thoughts are connected, that we drank of the same potion in a distant past and still ail from some unique shared affliction. Yes, perhaps some ancient rogue dynasty has our destinies crossed and a telepathic romance keeps our minds gently nudging each other affectionately, allowing our souls to steal a breath from each other's world before returning to their own personal affairs. It seems I can feel the pull of your gravity at least when my head is clear and distractions are at rest, calling to me through the elements of nature that express your powers in mime. But chances are your witchcraft is unintentional and my passion is in vain, and I am just a vague symbol left unnoticed among your mosaic surroundings.

You have no idea what it takes to suppress this kind of energy... or what it takes to favor another woman's face in replacement of your own. Your taste is unforgettable, and the illusion of your skin against mine is at times so concentrated that my body warms from the very thought. In my mind I breathe into your neck and sift through your shining hair, my desperate senses synthesizing the gifts that your tangible qualities have to offer. Your black cherry lips entertain my extrasensory perception, and at times I swear I can detect traces of your self-augmented perfume seeping through the mustiness of my chamber.

Even though it would be more grounded to say that true love better suits us in separate forms, I cannot shake the notion that you fit comfortably into a groove on some throbbing patch of my soul. Even if we were not meant to be lovers, should you not be my estranged step-sister peeled from the same mold on a more aesthetic plane? I feel familiar with the nuances of your figure even though we have only held each other in some chimeric fable now banished from time, and I know your kiss as if you planted it moments before I awoke. What a shame that my talents should go unanswered and your beauty be reduced to a single photograph, for so much wasted affection does not convert into clout in a demanding world.

It is true that rational thought allows more tangible lovers to cycle in and out of my life, but you will forever dominate the lonely spaces in between. Unless my destiny should be doubly lit by a sudden intervention, you will always be an unprofitable sugar of the imagination... for wishful thinking is on our side but reality is not, and my love is reflected back into my soul like light bouncing harmlessly off of a mirror. Sometimes the greatest love is more wisely spent on one's self rather than squandered away into decadent thoughts, and I would be more of a man to train myself from the cindering memory of your touch.

Noctiphilia

Sorrow eater, midnight fetor
Consecrate me where I lay
Day corroder, precious odor
Smother me in disarray

Secret prater, night invader
Croon to me in riddles long
Earthborn temper, daylight crimper
Drench me in atonal song

Spirit shaker, mythos maker
Resurrect my dying ash
Moonbeam longer, fever stronger
Potent where the dead rehash

Meadow walker, window stalker
Lordess of the silent shade
Magic keeper, sapphire deeper
Beautiful in nightmare made

Shapeless shifter, tombstone drifter
Wait for me at bedside drop
Umbra seeker, coffin leaker
Shadows on the summer crop

Season bringer, saccharine stinger
Wrap me in organic lust
Sweet injector, wraith detector
Leave me only when you must

Autumn primer, witch's timer
Darkness is a welcome sin
Mantra tainter, starlight painter
Dawn will steal from me again

To the Perfect Enemy

Unchallenged evil armed with flawless debonair
A successful crossbreed of deadly beauty, strength, and hideousness
With your fluid horsehairs draped over your sinister gaze,
You dissect my spirit and grow wise from watching my moves

You steal my knowledge and use it with ill intent
Molding a new dark entity out of my merciful intentions
Prying my desperate fingers off the cliff from which I dangle
Stabbing a jealous nerve as you expunge my existence

A malignant evolution's answer to the courier of a holy breed
The Devil in his most current form, designed to repossess my niche
Making the noblest man cower before his newfound envy
Using a primal elegance to make the purebred damsel swoon

Your sentient movements reek of intelligence and confidence
Spreading out into a one-man chessboard army
Matching wits with my every step and every breath
Igniting a cancer that smothers every aspect of my life

You prove a worthy foe, even in your weakest moments
A storybook villain resurrected with a modern edge
Carven likeness, soured twin… pruned before a blackened mirror
A fire alive since the beginning; infection of a shared past

Symbolizing mentorship meant to train the weak for war
Success of design equipped with an ill-beating heart of lead
Defying a brotherhood that could've been carefully sculpted…
A brotherhood whose origins reach far along a backward vein

Your fall is as sad, graceful and ironic as it is a relief
The vaguely reptilian glare of your eye surviving in a memory
A reminder of genuine evil that once kissed the face of reality
Leaving but a ghost to blister the backdrop of my imagination

Trespassers' Union

Mankind is a creature of learning; his heroes are seekers of wonder and his eyes are chambers of ravenous flame. Even the loftiest of leaders are not immune to the seduction of curiosity, lured into her supple bed for a night of unfiltered visions and uncanny inspiration. A sect of alluring forces selects its victims carefully... calling forth the sleepwalker, the spell speaker and thrill seeker alike; with legs akin to air they are led into the bowels of a wilderness orphaned by the gods of man, across sunless oceans and snow-spotted fields in search of trophies that would spark envy even among the closest of brothers. Weak are the dizzied mortals whose sole purpose is to bask in the ecstasy of primitive wonders, slack-jawed and teary-eyed at nature's vicious beauty... and strong is the bond between such wonders and the austere world that has nurtured them since their awakening thoughts.

Secrets in their naked forms, sleeping in some vaults and restless in others, house themselves beneath the amber plains in wait for those few brave inquisitors that stumble in the graveness of night. Whether their discovery is a product of luck or misfortune depends on the motive of their claimer, for some yearn to feel closer to the unknown while others feel content to shrink in its shadow. Whatever the case, one taste of exile can make any avid traveler turn his back on his home and bathe in the pool that is dangerous to drink. The audacity of such truants will lead them to scavenge on the remnants of empires now relieved of their glory, such as the salted pillars of Atlantis or the mossy, vine-veined tombs of the Mayans. Leaning to the call of some forgotten religion teeming with abandoned gods, they dirty the hands that push society away as they dig for ancient counter-religious texts... drunk off the fumes of mold-stained chambers vented for the first time in countless years.

The few that return will bring tales of bold rituals, dark knowledge and even miraculous beasts, only to be mocked by the sedentary man who has never been known to bid on a journey. Pity on the one who has never sprinted across fear's playground in pursuit of some forbidden treasure... for it is he who will never experience the most beautiful and treacherous places the winds have ever been. Only those brave enough will set out to conquer, and only those insane enough will refuse to return.

These lone knights guard eccentric wishes to be buried in queer places unmarked and unfenced, or to be reduced to ash and thrown to erratic winds that reach for every corner of the Earth. Though it might be against their mother's will, a traditional ceremony is not among their last requests. The dark woods, the lonely dunes, the frigid cliffs are their funeral guests... and what better song to pay tribute than the solemn silence of *terra nullius*? For some strains of mankind, home is not synonymous with a birthplace. Grabbing what few prayers drift far enough to reach them, the scattered explorers curl up beside cold stones and stern idols to be cradled by an abrasive wilderness; delaying the day when they will bring their findings back into sound light and tell their triumphs to the world.

Prelude to Lilith

Eve polishes the apple with a rub against her chest
And offers it to Adam with a beckon call of perfume breath
Nameless pleasures coat his throat, a consequence of scorpion sting
Realms no longer kept from man unveiled by fallen angel's wing

Cradled in a primal sleep, our hero soon forgets his quest
Locked away in goddess keep, asleep beneath the Devil's crest
Her scent is rain, her blood is wine, her eyes agleam in serpent make
Prometheus has no greater gift for man to break his vows and take

Dark Hours

In the late hours when doubt trickles into my lair like a nebulous ink, I bathe somewhat willingly in its shadow as I succumb to the rituals of self-reflection. The clock announces the beginning of its midnight magic, and thoughts as harsh as blades are free to roam unclothed... a spiritual journey not intended for the weak drops and spreads its bat-clawed wings. My karma is questioned as I approach the darker side of divinity... Notions of vengeance and other sins drown my veins like a deep, full-bodied wine, while the departure of twilight brings restless revelations to my doorstep.

A choir of angel voices sends a chill down my spine... whether they sing misery or praises is unclear. A symbol of hope forms on the face of darkness... but is this true hope or merely more trickery? The cloudiness of carefully blended omens surrounds me, immersing me in decisions of a biblical magnitude... My soul weaves as my fate splits in two. Chattering minions reveal glimpses of a hopeless underworld, warning me of delinquent destinies tailored for reckless mortals such as myself... On the other hand heaven's portal still lies open, though it grows dimmer behind the heat of frustration and contempt.

Temptations seek to embellish my sinful nature... striving to make me a cursed man yet. Visions of malice stimulate my inner child into becoming a larger, swifter entity. A stubborn man such as myself may turn his cheek from the angel's kiss, may shield his eyes from the demonstrations of miracles... and he will join the lowly shadow-dwellers in their self-inflicted peasantry.

The drug of sleep she comes and rescues me, purging me from this medial plane between heaven and hell; with a final exhalation I am granted passage beyond this realm of suspended souls. Salvation comes in waves of nocturnal detachment, an ample substitute for the pardoning of my crimes... for I sleep to find God, and I sleep to escape God, accepting oblivion as my master and domain.

He Who Remains

Death has made its most pleasant offers, taunting me from the mouth of a coward's exit with the painless erasure of poison fruit… but I have found the will to turn my back on the call and renew my courtship with life's simple pleasures. A warm bed has long been made for me in oblivion's cradling arms, but now that bed will rest a worthier soul given to a more honorable fate. At least for now life still holds secrets baffling enough to distract me from misery, leveling the scales once more to freshen a dose of life-giving anesthesia. Once again the droning timbres of night have filtered into my sleeping quarters to grease the passing of sapient burdens, and the reassurance of birdsong, however mundane, will greet me again with the advent of morning.

Fresh air will continue to fill my lungs whether I welcome it or not, thriving like an antidote administered when I was helpless to resist. I am once again fooled by the quick hand of happiness; furthered by the faintest idea that there must be some light at the end of the tunnel, some kind of meaning if not a reward. Do I dare to see the image of a child staring at me shyly from the side of a future love, symbolizing possibilities that may eventually complete the broadest circle? The higher I rise from my knees the clearer its face becomes, materializing into view with a spark of hope rekindling in its eyes. Is it that hope that pulls me back from the ledge and slips the blade back into its sheath, or is it fear? Perhaps fate has some influence over me after all, swooping in to save me like an angel that only shows its face in the darkest hours of failure. My place in time echoes some vague significance, resilient even in its infancy… This twisted tale still threatens to survive my intentions.

A battle between passion and monotony has claimed me in its crossfire, holding me hostage in a near immortal continuum that is as blessed as it is cursed. A new form of energy derives even from my oldest wounds, and in time my childlike hands will learn to shape it and use it for the betterment of my soul. It is not that I no longer nurture my submissive side; it's that I feed it away from prying eyes and shelter its wounds from a blood-lusting mass. Now those intermittent showers of rain will do my weeping for me, and the taste of defeat that rests in my mouth will soon be known simply as the acrid taste of being a man.

Welcome One

    Fleet-footed in dreams is a willing fool for the mind's magic, driving his steed at full potency through lands never shadowed by kings nor queens. He dwells where queer concoctions of weather make for an eerily peaceful ambience, and birds linger even when thunder groans portentously… where autumn seems longer than the autumn we know, and even the summers are sometimes hushed to an enchanting degree. His steed drinks from benignly haunted pools, and sleeps under a corpulent moon that hangs bloated in the sky like a botched pearl. Together they drift from wonder to madness and back again without the weight of watchful eyes, in search of elusive goals that wilt in comparison to the richness of the journey.

    Never diluting his nomadic spirit, he conquers new lands without marring the soil with a triumphant flag; hurrying on to new premises after a drink from a stream and a rest under the stars. The mouth of the world opens up before him, as he follows his heart deeper into an unscathed paradise of seasons and solitude. The elements in harmony greet him with every breach of the horizon, and a guardian sun follows him with cloud-softened rays extended reassuringly. The shadows of eagles cross the path before him, circling the upper currents with dauntless wit and grace, while trees that defy the seasons spill their mingled scents into the air.

    A turbid sea stubbornly awaits him, but his horse turns into a galley and its mane into a sail… as nature's opposition merely colors the quest with a welcome diversity. Out into sparkling stretches of blue and green infinity they glide, over roseate reefs and flooded gardens littered with golden coins from pirate lore. Brave dolphins dance at shipside, shimmering in the tonic sunlight as they leap amongst the seething foam… Shape-shifting clouds cast whimsical shadows upon the waves, with never the threat of an altering storm to impede the course of a one man crew.

    Stark white beaches greet him at shore, so blindingly pale that they urge the eyes to squint. There are no footprints to mar the sand but his own, at least none that have survived the tides. Inland orchards lure him further, enticing him to come full circle as he approaches increasingly rural terrain. Miles of trees heavy with fruit dispel any thoughts of famine, supplying a paradise fit for any refugee from reality… the curse of loneliness does not dare creep into his soul, despite there being no one to divide the wealth. He will forever be the sole heir of such flawless vistas; the emperor of every detail sculpted to his liking by a charitable divinity.

His path will never end in a grave... nor will it transcend a cemetery's gate with obligations to mourn... instead it only leads to one ascending staircase after another. Dense skies caked with auroras call him to his post, where he will survey his domain with the vigilance of a knight upright in armor. The exultant drifter prays to painted peaks alive with the tuneful echoes of incantations adrift, nestling into the arms of a merciful anchorage unknown to would-be intruders from abrasive outlands... The prevalent son of a dreamer's gold-flecked bloodline will never forsake his origins in the heart of an amorous universe, ever grateful of the natural gifts that constitute his spacious hearth.

Fuel for a Forgotten Tale

Seasoned fables traveled far,
In scent of moist and mossy stone,
Tell of dripping dungeon depths
And languid beast at teething bone

...Of ever long heroic miles
Caverns warm with dragon breath
Labyrinths etched on gritty maps
Haunted by unlikely death

Dynasties have left their scars
In curtain velvet, castle brick
Gently guiding spoken spells
O'er a thousand candle wicks

Eagles cry across the fields
Where years ago the wars were waned
Wars that burned where now is green
Wars that gave the fields their name

An orphaned warrior pulled a sword
With metal-clenching battle fist
A saddened woman sent her son
Into battle with her kiss

Legends written where they fell
Dampened scrolls in coffin care
Warnings hoisted by the old
Futile lest the young beware

Descendants of the eldest tribe,
With steely phantom tales in tow,
Drag their feet across the ages
Blind as ceaseless rivers flow

Now storytellers tell their tales
To children quick to lend an ear
To every other word respond
With laughter, awe, and gasps of fear

Fossils, tomes, and conversation
Boast of sorcery survived
Stories mold to newfound masters
Thawing with a pulse revived

But see, in time, these things will die
As drunkards scoff into their ale
These dwindling scraps will soon become…
Fuel for a forgotten tale

The Mercy Seekers

Wanderers they are, restless as the constant burning of great stars... Their paths checked by time and the interference of petty gods, they seek to isolate peace and sanity from the cluttered crimes of the world. Anxious dreamers but not wishful thinkers, they writhe in the agony of high expectations and the irony that often follows... their lips pursed with the sour taste of veracity dashed with cynicism and stunted hope.

I wish to help them, as I am no virgin to the afflictions of the mind and heart, but who am I to rob them of the morals that entail their quests? Every pain has its place, every tragedy has its enlightening moments. But still I pity them as I pity ghosts without resolution, and I would take them under wing if I could amount to the savior they are seeking. Is it Christ's touch that they are reaching for, or the touch of some more obscure messiah? This I do not know... but no matter, for I am just as much an orphan in this crowded world of leaders.

These wanderers... the mercy seekers... know it is both a blessing and a curse to love another, for once you love someone you are burdened with the task of their protection for life. To love another is to guard another, and the horrors of the world know this as they lie in wait. Unconditional love, it seems, is yet another treacherous road the mercy seekers must take. The weight of a man's heart is on his back, not his chest, and Atlas assumes not a greater task.

I have seen the paths that these pilgrims are to take, and they are flowered with treacherous things... Should you wander that way as well, take along your thickest skin. Anyone that carries a heart is prey; compassion is the soft, vulnerable underbelly that the cruel crouch to find. The colors of conflict cycle through their shades, from death and disease to devils and dementia. Villains of every breed carry Cain's legacy under a resilient black flag, stalking their niches like spiders waiting for a victim to quiver their web.

The trials of good and evil will come to a head; which prayers will be answered depends on whose master wins the battle. Empires will fall and hells will be vented, releasing the demons that have preceded the moment... And in the aftermath of chaotic disclosure, when the smoke of the ending days clears at last, there will be the mercy seekers... crawling towards their final sanctuary, heaven in their dying eyes, and the taste of salvation upon their tongue.

Show You

      I am your protector, your provider and your teacher; a newcomer bearing gifts unlike anything you've seen before. With a warm, outstretched hand I welcome you to my world, feeding your childlike gaze with my own recipe for awe. My intention is to whisk you away to a safer, more fatherly place, where the subliminal hum of a warm half-melody laps at our feet like the edge of a lagoon… Where I will serenade you with a song more potent and enchanting than any song another man has to offer, and paint you pictures more alluring than any dawn or dusk you've ever beheld. Not since the walls of your mother's womb have you seen a better refuge, for the love that I hold for you surrounds us with every deeper step into my realm.

      Your infantile eyes give my world purpose, give me someone to reveal my sacred inner workings to. I want to show you things not usually meant for another's intervention, things overlooked by an ignorant society. Pearls of wisdom, grains of wonder, are on our agenda for tonight… starlit beaches and summer-lit peaks await us, molded to our every whim. I am a dreamer, and I will show you how to do the same. I am not a god, but I wish to create in your name. A lion's heart credited to a more noble former self revives my ability to sustain you, steadying a lover's stronghold upon golden pillars of trust. Your joyful tears of innocence glimmer in the light of my nurturing heat, proving your right to inherit this kingdom I have bedded for you. Once you are there, no thief in the night can take you away… and no horror left from your past can take you out of my arms.

      I trust that you should not suffer any kind of pain; not in any world, not on any plane. Take my hand and we'll leave this severed pipe dream you tried so hard to save, and I'll take you to that place your father promised you in tales at your bedside. There you will sleep soundly in arcadian meadows while I admire you from above, sworn to be your guardian against the telic gloom you once knew before eternity was born. As soon as this flame gives out I will light it with our own. As soon as the boundaries of this life release their grip on me, I will show you what I mean.

Out There

Out there beyond the river that feeds a midnight vale, beyond the mocking cliffs that frame an auroral skyline, there flow exotic walks of life tread only by the likes of solitary warriors and calloused hermits. Out there the rains travel to lands untitled, rearing lush forests where untamed magic stirs in furtive form. Vagrant winds mold deserts littered with strange mirages, and icebergs ooze through gelid seas whose tides obey the lull of twin moons. Both foolish and brave have measured their steps there, beyond the lambent fringes of a homeland's maternal embrace... destined to forget the lands that birthed them and the women who named them.

Somewhere a nomad rests at the edge of a lonely campfire, toying with a trinket that reminds him of home... Elsewhere a shaman cackles into the night, chanting to an intelligent darkness that shimmers with the eyes of wild beasts. Somewhere a dragon sleeps on a bed of gold coins... smoke curling from its nostrils, protecting its treasure from would-be warriors who stumble into such sparkling chambers... and still somewhere darker, more obscure threats rattle their chains in the depths of caverns never warmed by any torch.

Morning mists part to reveal a red ocean boiling with the hues of the dawn, waves rolling with lips of redolent foam. The slanted shadows of Stonehenge, long and gaunt, lean to the sway of the sun, while wet jungles belch steam like factories in the haze. Enchanted fauna fashioned from forest myth, the proliferated children of various fits of sorcery, creep through unwritten avenues that know nothing of the death of magic. Castles and ruins tinged with moss stand like cairns unmarred by any epitaph, and tombs strange to the light of day rest heavy with jewels and relics in the clutches of frigid cadavers.

Too often such regions set the stage for my tired tales, but had you glimpsed such naked Edens in a most thorough trance you, too, would sow their praises. Dare I compete with seasoned storytellers in singing their praises to you? I, too, wish to testify that my heart belongs elsewhere... throbbing where mammoths rest frozen in the gut of a glacier or stone cities sleep in the blue haze of an ocean's bowels. Not every man's paradise stems from the tropics, or hovers close to the contract of company. Sunlight cannot parent every stretch of the world; courage begins in the absence of flame. I grow weary of my home and the safety it swears by, my spirit waits for me in places removed.

Behold

…And we beheld the beautiful nightmare,
That performed for us inhuman grace and strength,
And we gave it a name…

So that no man may deny its power and beauty,
Or forsake the intelligent gleam in its eye

Strange Nights

What fantastic reverie, what outlandish alterations of sanity these bizarre forms, children of Morpheus, mold from the extinguished events of the day... Behold, a symphony awakens where night does fall, emerging with its practicing notes to prepare for the night's vivid display of unfiltered madness. Sounds threatening to the untrained ear clatter and croak in a somehow enchanting ballad, a ballad that bubbles forth from instruments woven from all too unearthly elements. Ungodly rhythms tremble as forbidden sights wither and rise again, dancing in partially orchestrated chaos to the fiendish dither of rampant thoughts.

A wild moon mocks me, laughing from behind the green-rimmed clouds from which it sprang forth when dusk had long breathed its final breath. The dam between life and illusion thins into mere cosmic dust, as subliminal sorcery akin to unknown eras weakens my sobriety with an assertive godlike power. This temporary dementia, this gift from the mischievous sprites of darkness, arrives at my bedside to entertain my bolder half with a lawless pageant of deception. An eerie romance crimsons before me, while visions I never knew I had the power to conceive flourish forth from forgotten primal regions of the brain.

My anarchic mind, though free to roam outside the vanilla shades of my most prosaic days, will return to empty hands when the light of morning enflames the east... and confusion and ecstasy will taper off into westward voids that fade with the songs of nether worlds again forgotten. The entire deranged treasure hunt is condemned to be fruitless, despite the confidence of wayward energies once deft in their charade. The world of the awakened shines its sobering light where poltergeists once played, revealing nothing but the lifeless objects of a quiet, sunlit room.

The echoes of transient affairs fade behind my daily steps as the depths of forgetfulness quench the fires of experience... Where alien fabric had once caressed my fingertips there is now only the filth of my duties, and the heavens watch over me sternly should I deviate from my routine. But when the sun grows heavy in the west, the heavens will sleep and that dreamy dissonance will again creep in to cradle me in tonic vortices undiluted... Lord willing, I will stretch my leash once again, and to the abodes of sanity, I will bid you goodnight.

She Awaits

Eyes aflame with sapphire grain, my sultry mistress ebon-cloaked
Witch's queen and lover's vice, her hair reminds of raven's coat
Her crimson lips boast thicker spells, my incense-perfumed spirit tease
In wait for me in amber light, midst pyromantic luxuries

Dressed in shadow-melding cloth, her form sylphlike yet hard to draw
Shifty in the flickering light, her flux offending natural law
Her skin is neither pale nor dark; polite to touch as dewy fruit
But never cross her path with spite; beware, my friend, her soul is brute

Her beauty shines when sadness looms, her tragedy devours as flame
Restlessness consumes her bed, a full moon I am glad to blame
She tends to an erotic lair, a curiosa wonderland
Lit by slanted window shades and kissed by oriental fans

Flightless fairy, clad in black, her voice divinely resonates
Requesting me to drop my guard and lend my heart out to the fates
She slithers through the velvet sheets, a French composer in the air,
Lending out a finger curled, commanding with a demon stare

Labored with nigrescent opals heavy on her neck and wrists,
She opens up her curtained arms to soon begin this sacred tryst
Breath of cloves with hint of mint, a fragrance that soon greets my face
Her lips the color of her heart, her hair the scent of pillow lace

Time is not a rigid service, meaningless within her vault
Hours pass, so fleeting, as her tears and sweat reward me salt
Torch-flames tremble to the passion; vaulted roof, two lovers under
Unity of souls ensues, entwining to the song of thunder

Then she shows me opiate visions clad with necromantic zeal
I swallow them with wormwood wine; drunk, I question what is real
Her fingertips caress my cheek; strokes me with her dainty claws
She stimulates my weaknesses and enters through my mortal flaws

Her pulse resounds within my chest; my mantis lover takes control
I'm weakened to my very knees, unstable like a newborn foal
She leads me down a stairwell where the edge of darkness titillates
I follow her to drunk abysses, faithfully, where she awaits

The Right Shade of Pain

I am an apothecary of human emotion
I dabble in the art of mixing pleasure and pain
So many things to be wrought from the soul
Those who do not explore are not truly alive

I don't mind a little pain if it comes in the right color
I don't mind a little sorrow if its timing is right
Too much or too little may upset the balance
The balance that manages the fruits of my being

I frequent the depths of misery and passion
Drunk off the feud of conflicting emotions
The innate chemicals that bleed tribulation
Round out the sum of my daily feasts

Every gear in this human machine
Obeys its purpose without consternation
Not a single grape in the bunch goes to waste
I choose my weapons with diversity in mind

I have evolved the unlikely ability
To see the other side of this thing you call joy
A whole new dimension in mortal endeavoring
Teaches me new ways to ingest life's toxins

May rapture be the toy of lesser beings
Novices who question the nature of my taste
Apathy preys on the weak, not the restless
I escape into the mind's blue cellar, undaunted

I letch for the poison flood to my lips
The intercourse of undiluted banes
The collective wrath of a deadly assortment
The burn, the sinking, the drag, and the sting

My scowl drinks its fill as I sink in the moat
A swine at home in the astringent mire
Trolling for comfort at the strangest depths
Suckling from a vial of corrosive nectar

At times I need help to further the bullet
So guide these hands to push pins into my heart
I just need a touch of that insoluble twinge
The ache that signals the end of my infancy

Elixirs of love will never compare…
To the authentication of my crude existence
Restricted to the arena of self-defeat,
A funeral procession that carries me home

Solitaire

For some of us life is a game played by one's self, and love is an answer to a repetitive question that we may ask beyond our deaths. Not every soul has two parts, and not every soul that does will cross paths with its mate's. Our journey is long and our road erratic, distractions inevitable and vices enduring. Desire urges us on as we walk to our graves as slaves to our fantasies, our paths pebbled by destiny's lies… stopping occasionally to sample the strange fruits of boredom that hang so cleverly within our reach. Others carry on through a desert of false hopes, under the blazing eye of a god that fails to intervene.

Some of us fester in spiritual cubicles, so hypnotized by our own lives that we never know any world but our own. A would-be comrade waits at the periphery, but he is ignored in the name of stubborn denial. A fire burns in the homes of hermits and it is not love, but a fire that supplies a cold soul with warmth that he cannot provide. Cities grow large but people grow lonely, a contradiction that offends more with each passing age… Unity is not often valued in a land of weepers and wanderers, and heroes no longer obsess with selfless causes.

Our goals throbbing in our chests, we strain to see through selfish eyes… always struggling to reproduce our most glorious moments, always trying to make wine from water like the prophets that came before us. Things like focus and determination become vices as our worlds grow smaller and our windows grow dark and shuttered. Solitude is our master, and our longings are the shackles that he keeps us in. We squirm and rattle our chains until we are dealt by the hand of death… divided into our separate coffins, our heads humming with separate afterlives. The back of a cemetery holds a place for those of lesser fame, but not every quest smothered silently is a lost cause… True secrets belong in graves, and kudos to the ones who succeed in carrying them that far.

Contemptuous

Trust not your lover nor your leader; even your very self lays doubt at the feet of your judgment. Every character that decorates your life grins a grin of deceit, and every hero that pulls a sword soon finds himself twitching to the villain's tune. Join me as I thin the lies to find grim truth at their base, attaining a new level of glory by stepping over the bodies of defeated messiahs… to a place where our alter egos roam wild and unchained and our dreams are realized only slightly more different than we imagined. For somewhere between a spirited child and a bitter old man lies my soul, tampering with the chain that binds me to exhausted ideals.

For far too long the decision has picked my bones apart; to side with a savior who pardons my most ardent enemies, or surrender to the dark force that drives them. Finally a breath of paganish freedom marks the end of my vertigo, redirecting my blind desires to a place that waits contently just outside of nirvana. Tomorrow mocks me, but today I will drink wisdom unbeknownst to the passive lamb… like harnessing the power to ignore an omen, I sneer in the face of deities dethroned and steal the gift to synthesize happiness. Safe from disapproving eyes I allow my sins and lust to grow, feeding the fire that fuels my heart and mints the blade that is my soul.

But will I really be so brave as to die without an ounce of faith in my body? Only time will break such riddles, but one thing is certain… if I question my motives the intoxicating odor of independence will lead me back to the pinnacle where I found myself, and the crude paradise that I begat will suit us well should we need asylum. Here every man is his own journey, his own punishment, and his own reward, and lessons are learned rather than endowed by some divine parenthood. These lessons take their toll on their students, proving that the wise are often the miserable… but the heartless cannot be heartbroken, and the godless… cannot be damned.

Fluke

Life is a collection of symbols and quotes, but it appears a fog befouls me... How can I know their true intent when my intuition speaks in riddles? It seems the gods feed on irony, and nature no longer calls me an ally. Hopelessly spellbound, I am doomed to read life's messages without that precious third eye I held so clumsily and lost. Am I being enlightened or being hexed? These glimpses of ecstasy reek of a witch's meddling, or the wrath of some intricate drug devised by mankind's elite.

The forces assured me that you were my savior... Has my pact with divinity been desecrated without notice? Have I merely misunderstood my conversations with inner peace? My spiritual symmetry has been betrayed... The ficklest of fates evades me once again. You, my dear girl, are no more a heroine for my salvation than I am an angel for my enemies, and revelation holds for me no amount of joy that I had not previously grown immune to. I feel I have fallen out of touch with celestial forces, lost the powers I was only beginning to explore... Time has brought me failure, as well as reason.

I often wondered if you were that lone songbird calling in the night, a sole symbol of hope piercing a veil of darkness and silence; but alas, it must've been a fluke... a subtle anomaly of nature misinterpreted by a hopeful fool. I must be mad to have such faith, must be desperately drunk with dementia to think such foolish things. But I still want to know that I have a destiny, even if you are not one of its ingredients. I continue to look for signs in a chaotic world, carefully separating anything of aesthetic value from the general clutter of daily life.

The pieces seemed to fit so well, the story not without its streamlined beauty. It's easy to see how I could have been so myopic, but still I cannot escape the shame that comes with a return to the senses. But if you are not ingrained in my one true fate, why does your image still haunt me so? Your soft yet stern face, lost in thought, has become trademark of my struggles... but every clue preludes another clue, and it soon dawns on me that maybe you are not the element that is aligned with the ultimate truth.

No longer does every riddle sing your praises, nor does every thought find your face. Your spell is timeless but not invincible; I've found a gap in my circle of obsession. You shall join a graveyard of unattainable desires whose ineffability has finally been accepted, and your afterglow will become easier to ignore as possibilities prick me anew. But that is not the end of the story; your beauty still completes my cast of characters. Even if I am alone in this world, perhaps we have left our mark on another.

The Portal is Open

For a moment the clarity is haunting; the echoes travel the length of my spine to tremble in my stomach. Atrocities against time, achieved only through brief flirtations with blasphemous transcendence, summon forth my wildest childhood fantasies to roam freely in the conviction of mature fascination. The exotic screams of an alien era seep through to excite my ears, celebrating a sensual coalescence between worlds once divided… The portal is open, but not for long.

What rampant natural force or blundering rebel god allows me to walk the realm between rational thought and revelation, to indulge in such titanic miracles unthreatened by a dreamer's deepest nettings? The goliaths of an age unwritten surge once again through my mind's eye, mothered by some freak amendment to the laws of time. I witness a living monolith only through the lenience of reason itself, as I am stunned with childlike awe before a monarch of creation. Standing in the cross-ventilation of multiple spheres of existence, I can feel the weight of countless epochs pressing down upon my stone in evolution's path… It is only by the dilution of my limited mind that I am not overwhelmed to the point of insanity.

The future cannot compare to nature's greatest past achievements; a primitive world holds the trophy in maddening diversity. Soaking in the pheromones of the past for a few precious moments is the only way to taste what so many prevalent millennia have to offer, and witness privileged fauna growing unchecked that would otherwise only reflect in the eyes of a willful creator. Only a bold extension of logic, unapproved by divine counsel, dares to upset the graves of beasts once retired from existence by natural selection… and bring their forms back into the spotlight for the private viewing of my spirited delusion.

I do not feel fear towards this tear in the continuum fabric; instead, I feel blessed… blessed even though the gifts of unreality will not last long against the bisecting current of truth. Upon awakening I distance myself from the spectacle as though it were a pleasant nightmare, a vision of unique sensory indulgence that leaves only resounding waves of questionable memory. Images of extreme antiquity recoil into the dark crevices from whence they were first scribed by the stylus of the gods, and immemorial creations reassume their original archaic thrones in defiance of the means by which I bore witness.

Heathen Moon

The season is ripe with omen and the moon is robust; the natives grow restless and wary of the skies. They drink of the devil plant then don masks of an ill whimsy, otherwise naked in the bonfire's restless glow. Sacrifices of reckless judgment tinge the highest flames, set to appease dismal gods who may or may not show their peace… The significance of the fire is second only to the moon, although the combined light of each cannot bring comfort to this bigoted night. Drug-maddened voodoo rites dancing obscenely in the eyes of shapeless jungle demons that crouch far beyond the fire's edge… are a source of archaic intensity only hinted at in the dankest traveler's log, its gravest details omitted for the sake of sparing the messenger from condemnation.

Agitated by grim psychedelics and provoked by reckless traditions, the dancers contort their vaguely visible bones to essential rhythms that have haunted forests since the dawn of man. Their dead are present, though not in solid form, deprived of speech but not of respect… even the decorated elders cannot compare in rank and sagacity. The silence of the dead is as wise as it is inevitable, and their emotions are even more intricate than the ones that radiate from a beating heart. The dancers, too, are small in the shadow of inimical forces, as minute as the gnats clinging to the ceremonial blood spread across their chests.

Semi-intelligent spirits that see the world through an animal's crude intellect, blood-thirsty like the lioness and heartless like the vulture, gather to the chaos to be one with the tortured drums and other droning instruments. It is a sulphurous assembly, one where seemingly mortal men cast cloven-footed shadows around a frenzied circle of chthonian whim. The traditions of imps are the weaves of this spectacle, and those curdled spirits are crystallizations of the fury squeezed from burning bodies.

Wallowing in their entheogenic tantrums, ignorant to their sweat and their filth, the natives engage in physical blasphemies and erratic prayers that echo throughout the inhuman night. They exalt the shape-shifting flames, circling round the glowing camp in an abhorrent display of primitive motion. Even Amazonian rain cannot smother that voracious fire; the wetness of the jungle recoils from the orange mass. Seared flesh converts into ash, becoming one with the luminous coals that twitch with insatiable heat… Desperate souls rise in smoke, refugees from a tomb-less death.

How merciful are the clustering leaves that prohibit the light of those fires from seeping through, so that no curious adventurer may be lured to their origins and their possibilities. Some treacherous terrains slow the path of men for a reason, either to preserve the horrors of the past or to prevent them from spreading their plagues... or some half-cruel, half-gracious confusion of the two. But as strange luck would have it, no intruder could interrupt such a shamanic stupor in its peaking moments... the tribesmen would continue to flow around that fire like a venomous moat, babbling in unison with their priest to appease that bone-colored moon... the moon that ignores the forgiving deities of western civilization and shines upon the ruthless as an eye to observe without a hand to dispel the congregations of evil. Men of the litten lands, consider yourselves warned.

In Her Absence

In the blonde rays of sunlight,
I found the sacred grove told to me by my window

And I smelled the flowers and thought it was her…
But it was only a part of the game that she plays

She is, after all, at a crossroads with my mind
And the grove altogether is just a glimpse of the forbidden

A War between Wizards

I am forever a child of heaven-hell's hybrid appeal, teetering on the bridge between saint and sinner. I had ensured a seat of salvation in my youth, but shifting shape along the road to maturity has caused my fate to tremble. Innocence is fragile by nature, a jewel that becomes blemished in time… and I hold the tragic tale within me as a symbol of ironic transition. I had labeled myself a good man far too quickly, for I soon saw the day that my soul fell into the shadow of jeopardy. I now play my cards in doubt, gambling on a future that may have me in its icy grip.

I dodge at the feet of battling titans, striving to avoid becoming another casualty of the most enduring holy war of all… the war between God and Satan themselves. I am torn between two fates; too much meekness is suicide, and too much strength is the murder of another. Blood means different things to different people, be it war and pain or life and passion… In any case, the symbols of opposing sides often color my world, and it doesn't take long for the view to become crowded.

In addition to the heat of battle, there is wandering in the wilderness… The lessons that ensue come in many hues, treating me as a vagrant student immersed in the diversity of wisdom. Amused by the Devil's many forms, I followed him deep into purgatory's mock-motherly embrace… the lush, forbidden paradise annexed from heaven long before I was conceived. Like many confused souls I had become accustomed to hell's cycles, stunned by the intricate beauty painted by experienced false prophets, and I did not want to leave when salvation came to set me free. But an invisible guardian that refuses to show their face tethers to my soul, pulling me back from the brink of some frigid demon glimpse. Perhaps this guardian is merely a product of my imagination, and I am more good-natured than I had previously thought… or perhaps I require the grace of the divine to steady my route.

In either case, the battle for my soul trickles on as messiahs skilled in their artistry lock blades in their passion. The enemy's tricks are volatile, and a savior's touch is sedative, but still I refuse to choose a master. So be it if I should not decide even when omens are fulfilled and the revelations are upon us… I will not walk with either stranger if I must be rushed to choose a new home. I have learned to look to the skies for aid, but I cannot deny that there is still anger in me; vengeance is the one sin I have left, and it is the hardest of all to shed. Mortals are more complex than God intended, and I am no exception to the emergent trend. Even if I cannot so swiftly enter the gates, perhaps my greater half can be spared after all…

The Valley of Virgo

Before there was the beauty of a woman, there was the beauty of sunset skies and glimmering showers... and before that there were fiery chemical auroras and galaxies glittering with cosmic debris. The hours of man are young, and have yet to mold true monoliths that rival the significance of their ancients. There is beauty that is natural and effortless, and there is beauty that is desperately ornate to a trite degree... The artificial efforts of human beings often lean toward the latter.

What irony is it that Earth was so beautiful and untainted in a day so cruel and xenophobic to modern form? Glorious things once reigned where men could not breathe... nurtured by primitive atmospheres and shadowed by inaccessible oceans whose inhabitants knew the heat of the Earth closer than the heat of the sun. Thunder surged its way through that virgin valley, never to reach a human ear... echoing the loneliness of a deity who longed for mortal company. One day herds would graze on the grass that once had no enemy, though they would soon be damned by the renovating boredom of God... Some creatures would leave their bones, while others would fade away from the eyes of knowledge. Until then careful hooves dodged the delicate wildflowers; hooves that glistened with the dew of forgotten mornings.

The varied mating calls of beasts in heat weaved through monumental trees, and the hot breath of volcanoes towered eons before their slumber. No roads to scar the earth, no city lights to compete with the stars and dilute the night sky. Meteors went unnoticed as they painted their momentary streaks, for there were no sky-watchers to behold their dances. Creatures of night, dusk and day were the only shareholders of the land, and the raw witchcraft of nature was the only eventful interruption to silence.

The day the first spear pierced the hide of an animal, the hour the first man-made flame warmed five-fingered hands in the darkness of night... this was the day the sanctity of the land was deflowered, when premonitions of society slid down from the trees and crept out into the hunting fields of conquest. No longer could lightning upon trees hold the secret of fire out of mortal reach, no longer could fearful legend hold back the bursting seams of progress. A bond between man and his creator has been dissolved, the soil beneath his feet pillaged against what had been promised. Now wind scathes the lily face of a goddess once green, as she is exposed and reduced to a maiden ravaged... Cavern walls eulogize the slope of her meteoric charm, smeared figures telling the dole of her irreversible fall from grace.

Dunning Lake

I could see you walking slow along the shore of Dunning Lake
A black umbrella in your hands, a black dress flowing in your wake
Your reflection drifting slowly on the gently undulating tide
Obstructed only by the ripples born from black swans in their stride

Submissive colors dress you as to not disturb the lakeside fog
Your movements ever subtle as I sketch you in an artist's log
Advancing ever gracefully along the far side of the lake
The focus of a mural mist; a dream from which I'll surely wake

Layers of Me

For me, the self is more than a casket of flesh… more than a state of mind… It is a universe of mores and ambitions, and a lattice of experiences that replenishes itself from its moments of decay. An inheritor of amnesis, my soul follows me through multiple forms… uniting an identity throughout every plane of existence that I bend with my presence. Thumbing through eclectic pages, I encounter countless flavors of entity; waves of heaven, flames of hell… the echoes of birth, and the silence of death.

There are forces of nature specifically instructed to remind me who I am, even through eons of change blazing around me, and who am I to deny them the right to equal my shadow? They have been nothing short of faithful disciples, ensuring my place in the cosmos despite the opposition that doubts my significance. While I may appear from a terrestrial perspective to be blanketed by legendary shadows unequaled, in truth my being had already singed through layers of chaldean fabric the moment my fetal heart initiated its rhythm. My birth was not a singular event, but rather a prolific reaction that sent prophetic ripples through the eyes of those who loomed over my inception… and ultimately into the universe beyond them that serves as both a breeding ground and a graveyard for celestial bodies varied in size and rank.

As I step swiftly from life to life, I remember death only with difficulty… as compacted seconds in time, transient pools of coma whose sole purpose is to spawn subliminal inspirations that carry over into the subsequent world. My eyes are closed for a mere blinking moment, only to reopen to life's intricately woven web as it glistens in the light of eternity's creed. Memories are swallowed only to make way for new seeds of mental reflection… until I reach the glorious checkpoint when I achieve the mind of a god and am gifted to recall them all.

I am twice born, thrice born, and furthermore uplifted to the highest levels of transcendent survival, despite the occasional death of mere cells. Though you may never hear of me again after the lights go out on the life we shared, the voids will sing my name and galaxies will quiver to my presence ever subtly but ever long… I will forever taint the rivers of time with the salt of my being, a savior to my own interests and a carrier of my own torch.

Glimpsing the Demon

In the unguarded hours of night dream gave me a demon, one who had not been named but was worthy of the gravest attempt. The demon spoke in crimson visions; visions contagious even to the tamer thoughts nearing the consolation of morning. It promoted itself perversely as a link between my world and its own, belittling the sacred boundary between mind and myth. For a few starlit moments God's embrace weakened and allowed illness to enter my bare domain, questioning my sanity against the name of all that is holy and belonged. With squinty red eyes deeper than the trite symbols of monsters feared by children, it was an aberration sculpted for mature men... even the ones least prone to the imagination's more fevered tampering.

Beelzebub... Behemoth... Leviathan... Abaddon... in comparison all seemed like mere beasts of the wood, faithful to nature's intention. A transitory predator allowed to intervene only through the most powerful witch's unfaltering blasphemies, it spilled forth from the diseased darkness of a septic underworld to jeopardize my nightly solitude. Semi-amorphous, quasi-reptilian... the darker side of pseudo-psychedelia... crudely simian spawn born from the shadowed crevices of a madman's coma, bringing with it crippling shards of trans-cosmic hell. Disfigured divinity devil-promised... In its shadow I am weak, in its presence I am sickened.

But even the most experienced evil must eventually withdraw its ill services, for nightmares are as fleeting as the night itself. The ebb of black tides relieves the malicious of their sway, and I awake to the harmless tapping of a woodpecker only yards from my window. Fresh morning air parts the plague as the sun regains control of its kingdom, releasing my thoughts from the grip of scabrous talons. I am once again surrounded by things more luxurious than lecherous... Damn the restless hole to which the demon fled, and damn the feeble mind that allows it to return.

To a Girl with Green Eyes

Watchful beacons fierce and free
The kind so green as verdant sea
Of mint and clover sentiently…
Wrapped around your pupil be

Etchings on a radial gem
Echo to my deepest whim
Crystal carvings never dim
Further from thy pupil stem

Glistening gaze of dampened jewel
Strings along the avid fool
Not so kind, but not so cruel
Instead a different kind of school

Luscious is the teary glaze
That gifts me just beyond the maze
To gently whisper sensual praise
And rival my most treasured days

Subtle flits of dashing green
Shifty, charismatic sheen
Piercing through prosaic scene
Coaxing me to intervene

Sights aligned with passion's will
Sting me with thy lover's quill
A woman, lest my heart be still
As she moves in for the kill

Iris twin; an emerald pair
Tell of field and forest fair
Gradient of goddess stare
I wonder what thoughts may be there

The Wiccan Dove

     Young demigoddess who so coolly ignores my angst, queen of autumnal avenues dipped in golden twilight, won't you show me the path to nature's purest ventricle? I want to learn your pagan passion, and be part of your amorous druidism… I may have stemmed from the light but the more I learn about you the more the dark holds my attention. You are the source of spell, the mother of rebirth. Winter, fall, spring and summer are all one within you, for you breathe life into every realm that I am sentenced to endure. You are memory incarnate; you take me back to places that I thrived in, and without you those places are lost forever. Heiress to the mid-warm night, I am lost inside your Wiccan ways… and I have come to the conclusion that the mind that allows itself to forget you is doomed to ignorance without bliss.

     You are synonymous with the smell of fire on a winter breeze, and the crunching of leaves beneath the footsteps of a lonely bard. Well rehearsed incantations flutter through your head, and the dust of sacred parchments powders your fingertips. You have the evasive wit of a fox, the mystique of a wolf and the gravity of a raven… When you are silent you have the solemnity of a grave, and when you are outspoken you are blunt like a waterfall's hiss. The consequences of your existence have a severe impact on my life; without your birth my life would never have been the same. I need you, not as a lover in the traditional sense, but as a portal to a more thorough nourishment of the senses. I am jealous of your deftness in traffic with ghosts, and your audacity in spiritual exploration… I long to be by your side on those graveyard walks and dark forest outings too bold for the meager spirit, but it is all just a fantasy in more ways than one. May I worship you from afar, and utilize you as a symbol for my high-fevered longing? I promise I won't interrupt your precious planes of enchantment, though I want to be a part of them so badly… The least I can do is translate your world into a world of my own.

     You will never be true love; you are my obsession, my fascination. My love for you is childish, but grievous, and it rivals the restless longing that calls to the migratory birds when the seasons are in position. I smell the winter winds and wonder where you are, in the same manner that I wonder what archaic poetics decorate your book of spells. The inspiration I crave grows wild in your broom-hazel eyes, and the unique shade of salvation I require resides only in the aura you have created. But if it were possible to cage you, you would wilt upon capture… for you belong among the moonlit reeds where the night sky is your chapel. The wilderness is your only spouse, and I am in no state of mind or soul to compete with that! I am just as content with being blessed with your image as a tool for my mind; may it lead me on to braver pastures long after death's curtain falls.

Lorn

The Earth spoke to me one evening, and I listened as a child listens to an elder. Cosmic voices muttering behind the guise of cricket song chanted their integral spells, singing to the trees that seethed with the secrets of ages deeply rooted. The agents of the Earth could tell that I was lorn, and came out of the depths of twilight's circumference to soothe me with wisdom that could radiate from no mortal man. The hours grew long but not weary as I presented my dilemmas to the intellect of seasoned spirits that have never strayed far from the care of the natural world... An archaic symphony crafted during the birth cycle of time then answered with its organic dissonance, smuggling much for me to learn beneath the notice of other human elements.

The drowsy bell-tones of a wind-chime, echoing to the winds of a faraway time, brought me comfort and said, "Weep not for the luxuries of another world, for the loss of things awarded to you in another life... for grief slows the path of the heart, and the present is a fire that needs to be tended." The crystalline vocal fragments of a downhill brook tickled my ears and said, "Do not let things beyond your control render you sleepless, for the world turns on its own and needs nothing from you to survive. Who are you to compare a flowering tree to the horrors of war? Contrast is the oil that greases the gears, and balance dies and rebirths again and again." A finch, temporarily perched on an old wooden stump, chattered its musical advice and said, "Beauty is the missing piece to the puzzle, not strength. Your loneliness subsides only when you embrace possibility... Love is your friend, not your enemy."

Ever since that evening balm I try to unlock a deeper truth without exposing more than is needed, and without overexerting a precious natural ingredient... for it is only the human mind that makes a riddle out of an answer; too much processing betrays the product. But I am a wondering child doomed to sapience; therefore the question still writhes inside me... Why should it be so difficult to choose the simpler things in life over the profits of a world now dead? I suppose things that are out of reach are attractive to the troubled mortal, for the burdens of starving aesthetes are often candidates for cliché. Despite my doubts, the ghosts of reason's heyday lure me back from the maw of needless yearnings... giving me the incentive to stop chasing the woman of the past, and start chasing the woman of the present. I need no fame, nor glory, nor god-like power; I need silky brown hair for my fingertips... the kind fed by the purest of blood... and a sun-warmed neck for my lips to caress. I need to distribute evenly the pains of life instead of trying to carry it all in one surge, so that certain lines do not appear on my face years before their era.

Now youth clings to me like a successful spell, though I gloat not for fear of contradicting my newfound wisdom. The wet leaves of morning now hint of a new prophecy, one of greater value than the one that started it all. The sugar of a forbidden confection will no longer dust my lips; the cycle of a man in vain will no longer chisel my trials. Nature is not only a purveyor of complexity and tragedy, but a symbol of mitigation, rebirth and acceptance... Despite the friction that often burns between us, I will call it a foe no more.

An Angel in Question

You have silver eyes yet calloused feet
Ashen hands unwilling to greet
Your skin is soft but cold to the touch
Between your lips words have spoken too much

The strands of your hair are fragile and white
The sounds of your harp are insipid and trite
The song of your entrance is woefully crude
Wand'ring the heavens in a sullen mood

Your smile is crooked, your back is arched
Your gait is ungraceful, your voice is parched
You guard not a soul, but cling to thy throne
Your debt to the Lord makes the righteous moan

Not a kiss to moisten that weathering face…
That good men have pardoned with hesitant grace
Angel in question, where be thou wings?
Thou art the wife of a devil's king!

Dream Logue Two

My hand dips yet again into that treasure chest of woe, whim and wonder; that box bottomless with inviting eccentricities. Pandora did you see the breadth of this forbidden beauty? Did you inhale the phantasmal froth that I welcome like an autumn draft? Mortal men were wrong to chastise you on your discovery; you are not a burden as they say. I peer into that box with confidence and curiosity, as you did, and I see nightmares the same as dreams.

I am engulfed by the spectral assembly, guided by a sentient gravity that anchors itself deep within the soul. Longing in every shape and form pulls me in multiple directions; omnipresence is now a feasible talent. Inspiration crawls in the strangest of places; previously trivial matters are enhanced to distort the laws of both mind and heart. No sector of the emotional spectrum is ignored as the caverns of consciousness become alight and a primal fever enflames both the willing and the reluctant... I am no exception, yet I cannot choose a side.

I walk a sleepwalker's walk through semi-tropical gardens, my pores breathing the aromas of strange hybrid flowers... searching for the source of musically layered incantations that sing to me from sacred depths. Mystical forests haunted by the scent of pine cushion my every step, cloaking the mingled footprints of curious things both living and dead. In moments passed I see a fresh snow electrified by the moonlight, a luminous blanket that makes the night seem alive... marred only by the striping shadows of thin, naked trees.

I see beads of idle rain clinging to a window... gently vibrating in the breeze... and beyond them the luscious sheen of a cold, wet street, golden-freckled with the infracted reflections of porch lights. The mundane sigh of a passing car breathes a sleepy wave of white noise, bringing with it a curious flash of ominous fear. I know not the face of this fear, for it is subtle and has no name... yet it only lures me deeper into a network of memorable vistas sculpted for the eye athirst.

I take another step across chromatically poignant abysses, maddened to an enlightening degree. Chasms of darkness, chasms of light, all beckon to me with an offering of adrenaline that swallows smoothly and tastes divine. Am I intruding, or do I belong? Am I a newcomer? A stranger? A novice? Or have I made it this far before? It is no matter, for I gaze upon these ambrosial pastures like a warrior returning home from battle.

Even in death my trek never ends; it only deepens in hue and consistency. I have traveled more here than I have in waking life, and I've felt the heat of salvation stronger here than I ever will in a place the common man calls holy ground. How I ever dealt with the emotional famine of material life is beyond me; I learn more under the nurturing wing of a quiet madness than I do from the world's wisest leaders, and I feel closer to love in these alien shades of exile than I do in the brimful streets of humanity's reign.

In Debt to Love

It has been a long time since you've been the center of my pondering, a long time since you have driven my pen. How often I forget to extol the woman who taught me how to love; it's time to give credit where credit is due. You bring a welcome sadness to my life, a different breed of sadness that imitates joy. You are the sinking in my chest that dubs me a living creature, the sugary stab that reminds me I am real. Hurting you was the eighth sin, and I don't believe I have truly corrected my karma just yet... I am in debt to true love for chasing happiness elsewhere, and I received my hell well as I molded to the change.

Love is heavier than sadness, more focused than addiction, yet I tossed it around like a crippled plaything. This is a power I am not proud of, though it is admired by many... to gain leverage over love is to deny life's most static rules, but just as well refuse its most prolific gifts. It doesn't take long to realize my error in rejecting you, for I contradict myself more with every step. There are hells fitted for different crimes, and mine is made for the maltreatment of you... your tears are rife but I have not eluded judgment, rest assured that the fugitive has been detained. Your fall from my grace was worth a thousand broken hearts, and I owe their redemption like I owe a thousand souls.

It is too late for amendments, the venom has been injected... the jury finds me ungrateful and the night finds me alone. We are now children of separate worlds, guided by different songs and surrounded by different faces. Where is my sad little girl, with tears for me to drink and a chin for me to raise, who keeps the ice around my heart in serous form? She is in a world bound to bury me forgotten, where many a rose waits to outlive the old. So while you reinvent yourself in another man's arms, may you catch wind of this one final truth; you do more than make me whole... you have the power to make me human.

Dear Aesthete

Dear aesthete, have you wandered far in search of that sacred spark? Do your travels take you to joy, or do messengers find you in anguish? Perhaps it is too early to decide the nature of your quest, for your eyes are wide and hold many a prize. It is true that our pupils share many a mutual reflection; our desires have created the breed to which we belong. We are the clan of turbid souls pitied by the prophets and envied by the dull; upholders of the ilk that includes only the loneliest and most brilliant of men.

Every morning I must awaken and answer to desire… surely your day begins no differently, my ailing brother. When the sun raises its weary head we begin our strife to defend our case and outlive the arrogant voice of reason, spreading our wings beyond the realm of the blasé in hopes that we will ne'er surrender to the colorless flood. Dear aesthete, have you found the elixir that subdues boredom? Hear me laugh out loud as I ask you how to obtain such an invention… Do you see the humorous side of our plight as well, or does the despair of depravation overpower the fluff of irony's antics? Expectations so often fail me; the war against taking things for granted rages on. Only when you view life as a whole can you learn to love the day, and only when you are pricked by the thorn can you know your place in a tangible existence.

Dear aesthete, might you know that candlelight has a smell? I trust that you do, for that smell should not elude you in a den without distraction. The comfort of an earthy lair, curtains and carpet soaked with incense, may initiate the birth of your most potent apparitions… Dear aesthete, treasure those apparitions before they elope with the morning mists on the rise of a sweltering afternoon.

Dear aesthete, I want to achieve the kind of contentment I need to sleep without fear of wasting another night; a sated inner peace to cool the urgency of ephemeral life. The passage of time should not move me as it does, yet I cannot shake the fear that youth will slip like grain through my fingers. We must not ration our days in the fashion of the fuse, nor should we mourn the passing of our innocence… far greater things will come into focus should we allow our souls to ferment like wine.

And finally, my dear aesthete, there comes a time to put away revelation and return to the humble flow of normal life… to cloak the crystal that peers into the more alien regions of our souls… to stash away the pan-pipe that calls forth the wild forms of inspiration we see only once in an odd moon dance in its light. One must allow the mind to idle when a return to the surface is requested, however do not let the occasional lapse of beauty swamp your ambitions. Keep a page marked in the spell book of insightful discovery, but face the discerning day with newfound confidence and courage. Our illusion will resume to accentuate our ethics, and invention will return to finish what inspiration hath only begun.

Molding the Hero

He who is good shall go forth, softening the land with his good works and smiting the face of evil… sweetening the legacy of his family as he duplicates his flag for the world to see. This man saddens me as much as he inspires me, for he is a man that separates me from his niche and drinks a praise whose taste I can only imagine. It saddens me more how we struggle to preserve this man before his honor sours into ego… and we are soon left with a swine that rests grotesquely atop his riches. "How could you be so droll?" You ask, referring to my tendency to see tomorrow's villains gestating in the souls of today's heroes, "Do you not see the sun that smiles upon us in our victory?" I see the sun and I see the victory, but I do not see a link between this hero and me.

His blood reigns over mine, and his children will outlive my stubborn solitude. He makes for his wife the perfect wedding, and is able to provide a future fit for a royal couple. In his prime he is an icon unspoiled, until the bath of luxury softens the skin that shields against greed. He decays from a role model to a competitor, awaiting the chance to overtake my flock and dam the flow of my dwindling lineage. Despite his previously humane efforts he is still an animal, as am I, but we are different breeds and breeds such as us are often volunteered into competition. He is paraded, exalted and bronzed, while I grow sick with self-loathing and emerald with envy… Soon he is carried beyond his riper days, and they see not the ones he has trampled upon to maintain possession of that precious conch shell.

So mock me as you may as I sit here in the dark with my shortcomings, waiting for destiny to sculpt its righteous turns and lead me back into the light of virtue. A knight I am not, but the Devil will not so boldly call me brother… there is good in me, for I feel the efforts of its lingering embers deep within my pith. I cast a searchlight upon myself, flushing out the demons from the shadowed folds of my soul… plucking the parasites out from between the fibers of my existence. The foremost hydra's head turns to gaze into the eyes of one of its weaker siblings, inspecting the mirror for ways to better prune the entire swarm. To sever from sickness is to fasten the missing piece, making me whole again; balance is the ultimate goal when envy threatens to burden the scales.

I seek release from anger and fear; I yearn for strength as well as the compassion to guide it wisely. I thirst for true righteousness, not the mock variety, for fear that prevents you from harming another does not equal to good will. Sadly, my head is still clouded with vengeance even though the avenged have long been set free… but the walls of this prison are porous, as are all self-made conjurations that have haunted me since their triggered birth. These walls will falter when gnawed at with reaffirmed diligence, dissolving into a new day bereft of the clouds associated with dark beginnings. And as for my fellow man, his eyes will open to repentance when he sees his inferior gaining on his heels, and he will return to the humble seat where his noble plans had begun… thus proving that luxury is not always synonymous with decadence, and nobility does not always match timelines with rotting fruit.

So while that sword may remain in the stone for now, I will find ways to nurture those who take interest in my footsteps… cutting a path for children born from rogue wombs that share the spark in my eye. I will learn not to weep for chivalry lost in the mirrors of the vain, and I will train my inner child to wield the heavy sword of my destiny. I'll be reaching for the highest rung long after those failed heroes have slid down the ladder, and God help me I will achieve authentic greatness instead of merely feasting on the failures of others.

Into the Oils

Vibrant gardens emerald-gated
Private walkways lantern-baited
Fountains carved in marble piety
Hidden from an eyed society

Nature walks in colors stewed
Veined with thoughtful avenues
Lonely romps forever treasured
Peacocks speckle lawns unmeasured

Emerald evenings sun-enchanted
Fruitful trees dusk-orchard planted
Night unveilings firefly-lit
Bluish lawns where moonlight sits

Warm streetlights in puddles glowing
Streets outlined with runoff flowing
Tinted clouds where prisms form
Hazy skies beyond the storm

Cottages of homeland heat
Cobblestone in bridge and street
Houses built into the hills
Silhouettes of old windmills

Waterfalls of elfin size
Feed a scene for curious eyes
Streams that bleed through pheasant fields
Taintless where the footstep yields

Sunset stalkers credence-pearled
Lost inside a painting's world
Palettes of a thousand hues
Ignite an everlasting muse

Women Astray

They come for your heart... The false prophets of love, necking with elegant shadows in a serpentine celebration of curves and tilted light... Out there in the world of lady-killers and man-eaters, the laws of attraction never before seemed so prominent and cruel. What lengths would men go to for the warmth of a woman, had they grown tired of the lonely isles of self-preservation? Why, should they catch wind of the balmy hellions misrepresented by benign perfumes, they would abandon the very aspirations assigned to them by God. Courting the devil's daughters will never lead to matrimony, so if that is indeed what you seek then you must turn your eye to another beauty before your eye has so carelessly settled. Such a woman is never found far from vice as a shrike is never far from thorns... suffer a woman who has a cat's cerebration and you will suffer her craft as well.

Be it a damsel unwilling to be rescued, be it the vengeful mistress of a king... the female form carries many masks as she molds herself to the themes of the masquerade. She is quick like a gangster's gambit, clever like a woodland sprite. She is an angler that refuses to fail; her eyes are crosshairs of confidence barbed by lashes that provide shade for her ulterior motives... you can only see what she allows you to see, and you can only know what she allows you to remember. A trophy limed with shades of envy, she is a gem over which brothers are slain... minimizing the virtues of love, capitalizing the power of lust.

"Elusive woman, you will never mother my child, but you will restore my boyhood and prolong it for the endurance of eternity." ...Those were my final words to my object of desire before her memory solvated me to the core. Lad, she was proof that the poisons of youth may survive into our elder years... vexing us even as we sleep next to our wives in a fairy tale's resolve. Nevertheless – the curse of my weakness not withstanding – God bless the viragos and the vixens of our day, and pity on the simple fool who attempts to cross their path without the thrill of chase in mind.

Romance of the Winds

Winds are traders... bards in their rightful element... their traffic with the world symbolizes freedom and motion, even more so than the falcon with no brace upon its ankle. Massaging the oily waves as the tides tickle the valley's crust, these currents delegate their spectral influence over miles of prurient terrain; caressing every cheek and arousing every leaf with the leverage of the spheres. Electric sunsets illustrate the salty air... clouds marinated in vivid colors warm themselves at the edge of a sinking sun, synesthetic indulgences of light and hue. They taint the waters that gnaw at crimson beaches, a sister to the circuits of spring water that course through lush mountainsides padded with misted greenery... where canyon walls echo to the triumphant call of a saintly kestrel, the greatest prince to survey his kingdom's connections. The winds know those valiant wings, for they have courted them over a thousand bounds, and time will not jade a royal lineage so allied with nature.

Majestic sails bulging with freedom's gales tremor noisily in their tantrums, flapping as they tower over keel-parted foam in the midst of a rugged merchant's journey. He brings strange gifts torn from reluctant peddlers to dazzle kings and emperors in their prime, and the lands these objects meet will soon be permanently altered under their spell. Heaving ships onto foreign shores in the name of treasure-seeking is an act smiled upon by the winds... the winds that parallel the quests of merchants and seafarers on their undulating rambles... and in exploiting every stem of the compass rose they will follow the wide rivers over every descending weir. They wrap their coils around far-flung corners of the world, pivoting from coast to coast in the heat of some mission undefined.

I want to be in that glorious centrifuge, where the all-knowing winds of the Earth commingle and blend their scents into transitory potions that gather and disperse again. Aromas assigned to the seven wonders would flirt before my senses, passing but briefly as they cycled from one flavor into the next. What an honor to have your shoulders brushed by sacred transgressions as they make their climb to astral circles trafficked by forces en route... I hope that full scale omnipresence will one day embellish these diluted ties and unclasp my ankles from crippling brass. Being exiled from my flesh is but a small price to pay for a taste of places I could never reach with clumsy pedestrian strides, and I long for the day when my wings will be weightless and at last I ascend from my master's arm.

A Study in Sorrow

My disease... is that I want more than the fates allow. Somewhere between dream and memory my aspirations twitch and burn, where childish fantasy survives the stern scolding of reason. I have been willingly mislead into strange corners, following the disorderly tune of my thoughts... only to find that the road diminishes where time rewires my intentions. Now, the gifts of magic stolen from me, I confess to the rain with a pebble in my heart... for the subliminal clarity of rainfall seems to me the alleviating tears of God, and the squabbling throes of mental chaos seem to me the song of the Devil.

I am chambered here among my most enduring flaws and desires, chastened by an insatiable curse... damnation brought upon heartbreakers for their crimes of love, and I am not exempt from the wrath. I gaze into the mirror at the man who hurt the ones who loved him, longing for the day when innocence was ripe and inventive... but now is the time for revealing the chimaera, for exposing the outlandish and unreasonable; I am forced to trade my childhood radiance for the cold stones of logic.

My objective is to feed the ghost in my eyes, to restore health to the one who made my name a trademark of hospitality. Though age drains much of the hue from my soul, I will never forget the colors that inspired me in my youth; my deep-reaching roots refuse to break or turn brittle though my leaves have long since emptied their veins. It is the absence of that tinted vim that tempts me to turn bitter, but a familiar sound or smell that has for so long gone estranged will lead me back to the heat of the moment.

What a clown am I to obsess with things that are not real, to cherish so deeply things that never were... but it is such folly that sustains my life, and my death-bed will know those same trivial wonders as close as they were before. I would rather give in to madness than suffocate the inner child that turns the wheel inside me... for sorrow feeds on stagnant wisdom, and nonsense and speculation are a part of who I am. There is much to be learned from the dreams of fools, and fools that dream much will reserve liberation.

The Insomniac in Love

Passion grows restless within its shackles, renewed in form to a recent acquaintance; much time has passed since a fury of this magnitude birthed a spark in the depths and idle demons broke out of their latent gargoyle form. Her voice carols an angelic tone, spritely in its laugh and charming in its harmless sarcasm. Her name spawns an echo in my mind, and her scented profile leads me out of the depths of estrangement and into the spotlight of social candor.

But it is in the bleak light of the small hours that she inflicts her strongest sortilege, her amity flowering into a most ornate diabolism. She is innocent but her powers are not; she merely turns her head as I am eaten alive by her erotic influence. I toss and turn to the psalm of her pulse, broadcasted over metaphysical realms to find me a prisoner in my bed... Hours pass in the shape of moments when her presence lingers, deprived of her body, to chase away the mitigating ignorance of slumber.

She deters my evolution and reduces me to a sectarian beast; narrowed in the ways of lust and desire, consumed by the law of a restless trance. I cannot find sleep, dream, or even nightmare, only the boundaries of her aura that cage me in a pendulous cycle. I am biased towards her beauty, ever wary of her existence despite the distance between us that lengthens every night. She is my latest ailment, though I have never felt the warmth of her skin... It would be trite to say she is a pleasant poison, but no other allusion fits her as timely.

It is her soul, mind you, that is so inclined to devilry; I wish not to betray the benevolence of her solid form. In life she would harm no living creature, but her sidereal body eludes her moral confines once it is summoned by my juvenile yearning. Her righteousness fails her as the sun abandons the sky and the tides of passion rise to submerse me in a wanton telepathy. Night is our only time together, though we only see each other in the harmless light of the day's events.

She is dark but not impious, erotic but not vulgar, soft but not fragile, elusive but not distant. She is the balanced bead that rests between evil and elegance, the star that burns between night and day. Her flesh is sin, but her eyes are redemption. Corrupting her is only a nocturnal affair, and for now I may do so in only the smallest of ways. I call out, begging the spirits of night to bring her to me... "Daughter of Lilith, revived in the ways of good, open your wounds and let me in!"

Laburnine Lullaby

Moonlit grassland visitations
Waking werewolf incantations
Lullabies of laburnine
Songbook of the saturnine

Forgotten empire alterations
Atlantean life-force palpitations
Shapes begotten from the steam
Of transcendental gypsy tea

Agreeable gods with clouds at their chest
Exhaling into the sails of the blessed
Escorting ships beyond destiny's door
Lest they awake upon alien shores

Green-eyed sirens affixed to the sound
Singing of ship rats and pharaoh hounds
A thousand beginnings fresh in their wake
Trilobite tide-pools and lunar moth lakes

Sleep, my child, unwind your verve
And notice not as ghosts observe
Your mother cannot guide your quest
Instead awaits your waking breath

Grasp with lily palms the reins
Mischief flowing through your veins
Mind you as the moon besets
Sleep remembers, and sleep forgets

Wayward Spirits

Deep in the glacial crypts of the Earth's forsaken margins slithers a pilgrimage of morbid curiosity. Alas, the frayed adventurer who tires of the usual ark of entities favored by Noah's hurried prejudice and sets out to awaken widowing forces that will in turn belie his being; spirits that refuse the peace of a tomb and inflict themselves to wander, plaguing avenues of anguish and despair. Casts of darkness, agents of night… the dextrous elements of Hades rest in recoil, waiting for the shield to lower in a fleeting moment of warrior sloth. The symbolic figures of a dark tarot, native to unholy depths unblessed by nature's élan, line up to denounce the faiths of daylight dwellers in their eve of waxen blight.

Demons… like buzzards they are unmoved by filth and decay, grotesquely tenacious and undaunted to a vulgar degree. Stepping over gnawed bones, spear shaking in hand, our diverted hero braves their domain with reluctant fascination… carrying his feet across damp dungeon brick to reach a gaping room polluted with darkness and cold. A chalky pentagram etched across the floor, candles quivering at every angle, provides him with qualms that persist even at the strike of a match. What feeble light that survives reaches desperately into dripping corners webbed with unsettling arachnid artistry, but the effort is as much in vain as the priests that tried to expel the evil presence from this abode so long ago.

Under a drizzling skylight sleeps a cold altar seasoned with scraps of bone; ceremoniously disgraced remnants reeking of extinguished flame, aching to remind of detrimental rites once uttered to clouds that still simmer with their stormy response. The leaves of a massive book swell nakedly upon a podium like an offering, the weakened promise of its worm-holed binding allowing a trench to divide its uneven halves. A few pages have been turned by the cavernous winds that pass through, but the hideous spell most recently summoned is not yet sufficiently cloaked from prying eyes.

Iron chains droop over steaming dungeon wells, warmed by the rising clouds that still reek from the misted sweat of those who died in shackles below. The fruitless efforts of exorcists have failed to silence those troubled spirits; ghosts still electrified with the angst of slave life, arisen as the new tenants even after their masters have long passed under more peaceful conditions. What bitter sadness that a cruel man's death is a sated one, but hell only knows what degrees of punishment they may suffer beyond… even if the living world may never hear from them again.

Archeological clues slip through cold, gray bricks in the mouths of rats, the dissipating remnants of tombs pillaged and picked apart. White moths of unusual size cling to the walls like lifeless sentinels, imitating the gargoyles as witnesses to the unspeakable acts that echoed throughout these corridors. Only they heard the secrets that were expelled from the weakening bodies of captives charged with conspiring against the queen, and tortured souls had joined them in their dances beneath torch lights soon to be smothered.

It is a place solemnly perfumed with the lingering stench of fires now dead, save for those dwindling fires that contort atop pillars of wax. The newcomer looks around and sees nothing but grim décor tarnished by corrosive centuries... urns heavy with ancestral ash, candles crested with dampening flames. Now that there are no more prisoners to mark the walls, time is not a concern here... nor are the sun and moon, despite those miserly doses that peer through the occasional untended crevice. Strange that in this place the moon shines brighter than the sun, and it shines on the journey's final steps like a luminescent fungus. The warrior has come this far only to regret his gluttonous curiosity, for he comes to find that the only worthy discoveries of his pilgrimage are the graves... of his ancestors.

Against the Word

There is wisdom that counters wisdom that is readily at hand… new wisdom that is more fresh and evolved than the stale rhetoric of dead and dying centuries. I will harvest said wisdom as it ripens on the limb, awakened by the vapors of an outlander's creed that is destined to outlive the arguments of superstition. I am not an enemy of science, though my soul is not as rigid… I am respectful of the heretic's heritage but I will not adhere to methods described in books nibbled upon by worms and moths. The faithful student that is tolerant of his teachers may take a path of smoother stone, but despite my calloused strides I will no doubt reach a higher peak than his eyes have detected in the clouds.

It is I who goes against the wise man's word, and listens to desire instead… purity is not an apex that I thirst for. Longing is inevitable within a mortal's range; I cannot escape it and neither can the decidedly aloof. Welcome this longing into your soul and allow your heart to ignite with flame, for those who carry troubled thoughts with them to bed will awaken to unmediated novelty in the morning. There is a spring as yet untapped by the elders of any tribe, one that boils with ideas to be calcified and emotions to be interbred. One might liken genius to the act of blowing glass; distortion and heat mold great things from what was once a futile void.

You need not climb those cliff-side steps in seek of mountain monasteries beclouded by more than mists; no plant or tea thereof holds the key to your ultimate purgation. Clarity of the mind fails to impress me… The soul starves until the mind is filled. There are those who train to silence their thoughts, and there are those that wish to increase the decibels of inner turmoil… there are those that recycle the idols of eras now obsolete, and there are those that heed the shaman mirrored in their own eyes. Too many choose their poisons wisely and their cures blindly; escape when you must but silence will never answer the question.

To squeeze a prayer from the stubborn is to feed a contradiction born of reluctant submission… and with time this extraction can be accomplished… but rest assured that I will be neither the monk's apprentice nor the preacher's quota. As for me I choose not to meddle in the affairs of deities, for I see no victory in pretending to be at peace… I still carry a hunger within me, and as long as I am human I will act as such. Surround yourself with candles if you must, but tuning in to the din of spirits will only distract you from the voices that truly matter… the timbres that join to create your own.

A Curse Upon You

Many gave their pity or at least turned their heads, but you... you threw your heavy skull back and laughed. It was too hard for your face to fill my mask... for you to see the living world through the irony of my eyes. Shackled by childish anger and frothing with envy, I have waited so long for justice to come full circle as balance assumes position. Karma can be such circuitous witchery; the serpent waits so patiently to swallow its tail and complete the circle of ill intent... but when the wishbone breaks at last, you will be left with the verdict once intended to leave in *my* hand.

Then I will burden you to do as I do, cursing you to wander this world with obsession in your heart... and madness in your eyes. Gifts from the gods will be pried right from your fingers; sweet, dripping ambrosia deterred from its path to your mouth. You will suffer the scrutiny of seemingly wiser men, only to be mocked equally by the children at their side. Worst of all, matters of the heart will rash into a lifelong pandemic, and the thorn in your side that knows you well will anchor you down where self-pity stews in septic shade.

You will be sentenced to mourn in the lonely streetlights, ostracized to a steamy world of rain and tears. One night your competitor will swing around those same lampposts, testifying his joy and singing the name of his newfound love. He will dance along those streets that have become your private hell, for they serve a different purpose to a man whose luck has gone askew. When the night's events are done, the door shuts – the streetlight dies – and rain douses you with frigid mockery.

What twofold irony that your life will become the tragic comedy... a pitiful display that will drag on until the voice that belittles you in times of need runs dry. Perhaps if I caught some faint crevice of compassion in your sneering face during those times that I endured your disapproval I might return the sympathy in some picked over quantity... but unless I recall the subtleties of your nobler side, I will continue to demand your services as a jester. Daedalian circuits will reroute that stringent karma under the approval of the universe, for spite allied with reason is far from reckless verdict. Suffer well and know the symbolism of your sentence; misery will welcome you as an enemy retired.

View from a Coward's Den

Failure flows; I've met my match
Close the tomb, secure the latch
The time to reap my fate is nigh
The blade alive inside my thigh

Viscid devils conscience-sent
Origins of punishment
Mortal flaw, a deadly vice
Vengeance has its closing price

Beaten down from walking tall
Sentenced to a serpent crawl
Demoted with a beastly grunt
Reduced to a hyena's hunt

Character defoliation
Anxious fall in trepidation
Evil spirits at my throat
Shelled within a sinful coat

The price of mixing right and wrong
Weaving to a bastard song
Restless as the timid wren
'Tis the view from a coward's den

She is Legend

She is the one I speak of, but not the one I have seen... Or have I? She is not a ghost, but she is not truly tangible... Or is she? Questions of faith surround her; she is made of both wishful thinking and dying rumor. Every now and then a song resurrects her, but it is all soon lost in the death of a moment. With the stealthy power of an urban legend, she breathes life into the mysticism that has for so long been in drought... redesigning a youthful faith in things so feverishly imagined... but alas, shortly after she wilts before reason. She fans and withdraws like a colorful ocean polyp, vivid in hue but more fleeting than the land flower it attempts to imitate.

I cannot paint her, for she is woven of an ambrosial fiber that evades the steady eye. Her inspiration is the kind I cannot fully embrace, though I am allowed to dip my pen here and there. She is an undeserved halo that clings to my mind, hovering among my deepest thoughts without crossing shadows with my waking path. I am tempted to call out to the void, "My lover from another realm, more fleeting than the dust off a moth's wings, are you a mold for a conscious substance... or are you just here to tease me with your effigy?" I cannot domesticate what is not real, but I long to know her purpose in fueling my infatuation.

Surely I am not mad in the name of my pursuits; does not every man dream of the ideal woman, and search for her in every corner of this world 'til he is dead? I boast that mine is the most divine... although, as a price, she is also the most difficult to produce before the skeptic. If death shall find me sooner, perhaps she will be waiting there... if not with open arms then with a friendly gaze that receives me just as well. Until then she eludes me as the stars elude the ardent vessel, a constant of the horizon that remains out of reach for a seemingly eternal chapter.

To you she is nothing but the byproduct of a fool's thoughts, but to me she is the countess that rules the world of my youth and carries the antidote to my ailments in her life's blood. What a pity that her life's blood does not flow in this world... I shall find the world where it does, and savor it 'til it transcends to the next.

Home Beyond Home

From the dark voids to the lantern light, the tides of wonder stretch to wet the heels of would-be victims wandering along the beaches of curiosity… soon to pull them into the fury of colliding worlds and knight them as explorers of the infinite. Stories unfold, only to be told amongst the ones that wander death's terrain and behold its unexpected secrets… It is us, you see, who are to uncover such marvels and tamper with the doors that nest in sweet oblivion.

Outside life's farthest corners our purpose is not so unclear, and a grave is more pivotal than final. There will be journeys waiting beyond the wall… some will be taken in the company of others, and some are meant to be taken alone. In the dark seasons we will be separated from our loved ones, only to be reunited with them once again… Grueling lessons will be wrenched from stretches of solitude, and rewards await those who return.

We will be double agents to the dual branches of afterlife, playing both the part of the restless vagabond and the part of the idle hermit. No earthly belongings will burden our backs, for all that we need flourishes in the lands that beckon. Every night a new innkeeper greets us with a key, until we find another path that remembers home's open gates. Lovers oceans apart know that patience leads back to reunion, just as veins lead back to the heart, and fate owes its namesake to the act of making ends meet. Until they do time spreads us out like grains of sand under his fingertips, taking full liberty in maneuvering our rooks across the board.

Upon being exiled to strange arenas of creation, we will treasure the crisp scent of autumn fires for it reminds us of our home. One day that smell will lead us back to our mothers… back to our fathers, sisters, brothers… back to our elders and our offspring, to our cabins and our comforts. Villages rich with motion and being welcome the end of our circular journey, topped with fragrant chimneys and homely weather-vanes that trademark the world that reared us. All structures exclusively serve a nostalgic purpose, for even the graveyards are immune to sorrow, and spirits accompany rather than haunt.

What a joyous day it will be when faith is no longer blind, and hope is no longer an echo without an answer… but that day is merely an oasis in the underworld, a water-hole in a desert of wanderings. Despair not; wanderings are not aimless if they are fruitful, and the life of a traveler is not necessarily without its virtues. Even salvation must defend against boredom, and soon it is time to move with the seasons.

I'll Forget You Yet

At last with my back to your kingdom of longing,
I'll finally break free of your cycle of heartache…

And discover new realms beyond long-awaited death
Where I'll bask in the glow of a merciful sun

Riding atop some grand phoenix,
The brisk wind through its feathers and to my face

Over deep canyons of colored rock
And antique forests dipped in an autumn bath

Scanning steep hillsides and impossible peaks
Valleys that embrace no adjective but breathtaking

There I will find new solace in exile,
Independent of your magnetic core

Distracted by newfound wonders,

I'll forget you in heaven…

I'll forget you yet

The Lost Art of Sanity

History speaks loudly of the aberrant mind, caroling the praises of oddity as the anthems of emergent prophecy; the wind-scattered seeds of genius give bloom to new faces of contribution, each subsequent brainchild more instrumental than the last. Legend boasts that each time a womb bore a madman a villainous leader quivered on his throne... having been given word from the stars that his tyrannous reign would soon be overthrown by a gifted radical destined to reach his peak. There is no doubt that the climate bends under the presence of rebel spirits, even when unstable thoughts are restricted to mere canvas and clay.

The lantern light flickers late in the window of the avid tinkerer; still burning strong as his thoughts grow strange upon entering the weary hours. I can only guess at what masterful plans perspire from his cortex on such quickly approaching mornings, or what tangential fantasies hinder the progress of the creations he has idling in the blueprints of speculation. Surely we share the same father in heaven, though one is more apt to seek counsel in maverick intuition when the fruits of daily life grow ill in the light. Even if we shared the same earthly mother before entering this world, I still might not capture the spark that favored him during conception.

Few events are more addling than the marriage of nightmare and dream, and saints moonlighting as madmen indulge in this alchemy with hopes to parallel the brilliant minds hinted at in their scriptures. They are discouraged to find that a leashed man may only reach so far, and the temptation to abandon their original doctrine for the embrace of phantasmal love can lead to a dichotomous settlement between realms. A sane man is a man of earthly attachments, and he is likely to taper off into the abyss if he never learns to surpass his own psychic reach.

I almost pitied the words of the mundane and unstirred as they spoke their last breath on a death-bed of regret, had I not known the revolution that approaches; let them sleep restlessly and without their chains, for then will they know the mind's unraveled bounty. Be forewarned that the song that plays at the onset of your death shall not endure with its torpid symbolism and mournful irony, but instead shall give out like a weakly rooted flame... to ready a space for the next world that promises a flagrant entrance.

As for the world of the living, reckless beauty will not be bound by the walls of verbal description. When these wondrous thoughts do find a host, they will be coveted by those whose imaginations fall shorter than their limbs of reason. From sought after Tesla papers to dreams unrecorded, fevers of genius are envied to the extent that many employ some method of chemical escapism… a cheapened bypass frowned upon by defenders of authenticity. But despite the fray in the route of transfluent innovators, a common theme – one that supersedes the prosaic gifts of love and humanity – is agreed upon. For the price of beauty is not your dignity, nor your trust, nor the welfare of your heart; the price of true beauty… wild and pure… is your sanity.

Hermit's Eden

Put me in a home where the rain drums gently on the roof
Mumbling the secrets of a world subdued yet so aloof

Put me in a home where the spirits are at peace
Just another generation welcome at the family feast

Put me in a home where the walls and floors make creaking sounds
Antique percolations of an ancient vim that still abounds

Put me in a home where a hound is sleeping at my feet
Dreaming parallel to me as I drift off in my seat

Put me in a home where a clock is just a decoration
Not a way to monitor the passing of my jubilation

Put me in a home where a stained-glass window lights the stove
Open so the smell of forest meets the smell of spice and clove

Put me in a home where a fountain's rim is lined with birds
By day alive with cardinal song, by night foretell the raven's word

Put me in a home where the garden's always overgrown
Dogwood shedding on the gates, willows wept on stepping stones

Leave me, when the day is done, in silhouettes of manors arched
Candle-dotted windows; an oasis lit for travelers parched
Evenings oak-tree shaded welcome reinventions of my youth
Garden mazes tempting to the eldest living backyard sleuth

Put me where there is no rogue to quarrel with enflamed intent
Save for one familiar soul; a wall-adorning mirrored gent
He alone, the steward for a weary hermit coming home
Returning from an arbor romp, the farthest that I'll ever roam

Sympathy for the Abyss

One evening I dared to glimpse the mellow voids of a neglected utopia, drawn to its tattered curtains and crumbled columns so peaceful in their self-inflicted shadows. One tired night I dared to meddle in their mourning; a night too exhausted to near the lost apex of happiness and its forgotten fields of joy. I confess that I willfully tended to the sorrows of a hidden universe, intoxicated by its melancholy spirit; the opaque sadness that embraced me and held me close to its breast, tempting me to smother myself with milk brewed solely for the dead.

An exhalant decrescendo poured a dying sigh that flowed throughout the lower caverns of my heart, and I surrendered to a moment of misery upon being humbled before the bringer of ill tidings. The window to solace was clouded, so I looked away. The orchid of happiness was not yet flush, lying beneath the unbroken winter with the patience of a northern season; pleasures remain stowed away for another day. Instead I stole a sip from that gaping well and made the wasteland's pain my own. My languid pulse echoed against humid stone walls, syncing me with the lesser legacies of a ghostly kingdom that saw many failures follow its victories when its roads were warm with life.

The smell of flowering fields wafted through the moldy ruins of a time-swallowed city, and the citric spice of emotional contrast was welcome as its timing was adroit. It was a harmonious complement, like the smell of rain on a beach... an indescribable aroma that was as soothing as it was dank. It was not the first time I had seen gloomy worlds backlit by paradise, nor was it the most memorable... but it was a sourness that would welcome a far sweeter nectar to carry it down my throat. I was foolish enough to wipe clean the dust and open the story... the story of that wilted Babylon of glory expired, demoted to a crumbling land-reef whose intricacy was its only vestige of grandeur... and the emotional exodus that left it behind, more sadly spoken than that of Rome's descent. However, like many stories of this girth, the book came with a cover and a clasp to reseal its seasonal slumber.

Even to this day the purpose of that temporary ceiling eludes me, but I know it was there; pain melds beautiful weapons, powerful weapons, curious devices that help me focus on the finite scripture of destiny. There need be no reason for this sudden trough in a series of peaks; a man merely needs an occasional dose of sadness to keep his aura well-rounded and its colors rich and full. Despite what questions it may raise, that is my excuse for gazing upon the barren... A glimpse of sorrow is a glimpse of wisdom, and a soul unpunished is a soul untaught.

Fallen (Into Place)

It is a wonder how life contradicts itself with such grace, and how guardians led astray always seem to find their way to back to their post. I have taken many strides in search of a multiplied transcendence, an allowance to stroke the lustrous surface of well-being in defiance of the ones that uphold the fleece out of reach to peasantly fingertips. At last I reap the profits of seeds I had planted so long ago in once recumbent soil, the balminess of gentler days having finally ignited their vitality.

The steed that hoists my salvaged carcass will brave any marsh or river, carrying me to sacred ground I never thought I'd see alive, and the moment the horse kneels and leaves my body on the shore is the moment that I am gifted unto new lives inherited through a heart revived. Minstrel, play no longer your placid song of sorrow... turn your instrument of atonement into one pitched for triumph! Fear not, the clouds will finish parting once you begin your new song. As your notes begin to weave my being is rethreaded, the pieces of my doctrine rescued from the flames and refastened before a single letter has been singed.

The so-called "ides of March" did not carry out their prophecy; the black dawn dilutes as the snake eye thins from the valiant light. I pierce the shadows with renewed purpose, reconnecting the broken chain that constitutes my path of glory. It is a great feeling to engage in things that feel as though they were meant to be; fulfilling destiny is an irreplaceable high. A synthesis of positive and negative forces educates me beyond the ignorance of pleasure-seeking infancy, and I am awakened to see the beauty in truth and the hope in tomorrow's eve... no longer am I cursed to mull over the gift of life with helpless eyes bereft of a self-reliant spark.

Today fate is a woman... a forgiving and uniquely beautiful woman... the likes of which my life has never seen until this dawn. She tilts my head gently and hangs the keys to prosperity around my neck, granting a wish that has addled me since the first days of youthful aspiration. With her approval I have combined karma and grace to achieve new levels in conscious liberation and break away from my cycle as a student of ineffectual spells... Evil no longer desires my services, for my newfound halo has crystallized and testified to the reprise of a good in me that almost died. I have left no grove unfathomed in my search for utopia, and now the wastelands are moist with bloom.

Two Rivers

Envision with me, if you will, a pair of rivers running through the same land... one being the path of the loved and the other being the path of the lorn. Travelers on both sides of the divide seek equal footing... accompaniment through the extremes of this life, to heighten the pleasures and soften the pains. Eros surely marveled at the creation of his swarthy passion-drug as it glistened *in vitro* before him... and he would not be about to let this precious serum fall into the hands of any knave, thus the separation of castes. A fool would implement it well, and the naïve would best exploit its abilities. However, it is also a fool that denies its power, and naïve is the one who fails to honor the necessity of its invention.

The vehement, soulful stag sleeps with his back to love's warm flesh, lest unwarranted desire awaken him in the night with amorous pulls on his heart... However he is likely to expose his lips to the damsels in his dreams. One might not so easily grease himself through the grasp of spring's ritualistic allure... although there are bound to be some oddities unrecognized by the symphony to which worthy beasts are paired off. Then again, even renowned lovers may appear to themselves to live life in heartache, for the eye of the beholder is a governing force in the dealings of love of self or another.

How quizzical that both the eremitic and the prolific should walk different paths yet sway to the same migratory pull; birds maddened by the seasons' clock surely know a similar witchery, and many of them, too, fall in a feat played out for a mate. Irony has not spared the schemes of the heart from mockery, just as princesses wait patiently for warriors denied a return from battle. Still, they are in love, and they are blind to the tragedy that swears to distance their fates.

Lovers who have found one another have no pity for the heartbroken, nor do they have memory of their own heartbroken worlds they left behind. But whether or not they recognize the forlorn, their souls are woven from the stair-steps that led them to be who they are, and their blood is forever mingled with the tears of their weeping counterparts. After all, what is the difference between a rose for a bouquet and a rose for a grave? Only the purpose, not the variety.

Matters of Time and God

From the hopeful tears of those seeking out companionship in more celestial corners, to the dry eyes of those with their gaze turned down towards the Earth, there are many who question the routes they are given. Many look down at their cards in dismay, or do not realize what hand they are dealt until it is time to spread it before them. If you are like me then you have slept while the cradle crumbled around you, then when you woke to your new surroundings you cursed the one who moved you in the night. Where is the one to blame when there is no blame… the one who fathers seas to fill the gorges, and winds to dust the fields… or the one who keeps pace as our pendulums swing closer to death and our clockwork kindles piles of rust? It appears our god adheres to a chameleon's code, more obscured everyday that the world is in motion.

Time and God, are you one? Whichever culprit I am speaking to, I cry out, "How dare you renovate the world I had grown to love? I had not a chance to complete my tasks in the era I left behind, but you impatiently awakened me from that perfect dream." But I am wary to bet that the skies are listening. Who else feels the tremors of my heart when it quakes with longing for beautiful places now buried? Certainly not the one who digs my grave and kicks sand on those memories as we speak. Change is a worthy foe, and since the rifts of my birth his master plan has been to catch me unprepared for battle. Gills to lungs, worms to moths; the most glorious cycles of life seem to mock me as I watch loves and companions thin to a wraithlike viscosity before fading away forever.

Who is this nebulous titan that he should arrange the contents of my habitat so stoically? Am I a product of his rib, as woman is said to be from mine? Surely if he is the origin of man then some trace of flesh must tinge his sacred root. After all, even if God does not know the pain of love, he must know the pain of loneliness… therefore he is semi-human, while some sensations remain exclusive to mortals. Despite the scars he shares with his creations, he is intent on remaining shrouded in mystery; one with nature and the austere obscurity that often blooms in its palm. His voice is only in riddle, his face only in sign. Frustration grows within me as I attempt to call him out from his surroundings, shouting an extension to my previous offense… "Are the will to love and the will to create truly drawn from the same vein? Or are there separate forces at work, each oblivious to the other's task?" I yearn for some kind of deific solvent, to deaden these grueling tests and reveal what is to be the core of the promise.

We deny God everyday yet seek his comfort in the night; perhaps we are merely weakened by our dreams, our heads murky in the baffled light. However cold lay oblivion's gaze, I must find a way to gather its focus… for even in the light of day I cannot hold a fist forever. If I cannot find a god in the eyes of time, then I will conjure one from the very primal fumes of my imagination… the world of man will call this god what it may, but that slur will not deter me from my place at the foot of her throne. I will not charge *my* God with the murders accredited to time's changeling ways; instead I will redraw my God with the rogue face of impetuous woman!

In Another Life

...And I lost you in that gloomy world; our lingering tragedy finally came to a close. You left me covered in tears, left me to nurse a pain so deep and real... we were but children; how could the forces have been so cruel? Our love had no time to grow, but it was potent for a love in such a stage. Regardless, the early chapters of our life together were heavy and dim, and for the time being our love could not cure your mortality.

The shores of time slowly concealed our aching tale, and I was forced to forget you for my own health... but in this new life we are reunited, reminding us that lovers divided by death can find each other once again. Patient eons have come full circle, and dawn awakens me as though the bitter night had never come.

Though most of the stringent feelings have faded with that forgotten era, I can sometimes still find that pain lurking deep within my cluttered heart... waiting to resurface at least for a moment and cut me down to mortal size. Forgive me for toying with that succulent thorn, for rehashing that tearful romance; my life has long since progressed yet I cannot forget the taste.

Even my current joy is mixed with an ancient misery's residue, but I am ever grateful that I laid eyes upon you again. Who knew that our love could transcend such rigid laws of nature, and travel across impossible oceans of existence? Unimaginable mercy has blessed you with a sacred immortality... Lover, you will never again endure a fate where I cannot follow. Though we have parted ways once more, it is not the same sorrow; we now know the confidence of future meetings, for our rendezvous' will always have merit and your rebirth will never be in vain.

Beauty in Brown

Beauty comes in different forms
From prism glass to twilight storms
Rose's thorn and diamond's edge
Sunset view from mountain ledge

But blue-fumed coals at fire's feet
Cannot compare to woman's heat
There'll never be a lustrous pearl
That stares as deep as brown-eyed girl

Striking a Nerve

It has been years since that strange aural glow paled inside me, and with it departed the narcotic kiss of paranormal eloquence that had been so generous in sharing its warmth. I unwillingly shed a layer and left it flirting with the outskirts of emotion… left it to dissolve in the insufficient yolks of my life's rerouted endeavors… and even as I write these words I tremble lest it should never return with original force. Since then I have been looming a lifelong craving out of a single flickering whim; to move the stone from the river and let afflatus flow once again… to tap the golden vein and drink the sacred channel no longer inhibited by resistant forces. A deft euphoria… a thinking man's hearth… an ecstasy so unlike the culmination of a binging man resounded as my anthem. Gazing up through the angled mirrors of an unlikely perspective, gray skies never looked so alive.

The only crystals I am privileged to keep from that quarry of forbidden knowledge are a few intriguing realizations… that there are soft spots in my soul I never knew I had, and there are feelings within me that a lover cannot awaken. Angels speak volumes of this kind of revelry… the heavenly dream-state of bedridden madness… the luxury of being too deranged to fit into the rat race, instead reassigned to the toxicity of thought with minimal obligation to the outside world. Precious is the pyre gathered to honor the indescribable; cryptic yet pure, frail yet compelling. I wish only to be returned to the arms of my own personal kilter, even should I have to pry them open with overzealous extortion.

Oh, nameless feeling come back to me… come back to me in the belly of thunder, in the heart of the golden fall… but assure me that you are more divine than each element combined. Despite your strong presence in my life I have failed to create a name for you; no title seems suitable for your ingenious design. You are the child of nature beyond nature, but you are more mature than the seas that bathe this world. All this time you were not one, but many colors of consciousness… the endless phases of sculpted sanity that refused to stagnate despite frequent lapses of accessibility.

It is true; I spend more time clawing at the edge of genius than I do solidifying the inspiration I work so hard to unveil. What I seek blooms but has not roots… despite the truth behind its beauty it is sadly never to be anchored with substance. The resin has grown stale, but the memory of hopeful absurdity is still warm like a pearl cupped in my hands. No peasant maddened from tainted grain could brandish the thoughts that danced before me when that strange season was at its peak, and only the deepest troughs of delirium could spawn the portal to bring them back.

Then and Only Then

A man grew weary but refused to die, and he fought his way out of the tangled sheets of his death-bed. He kindled a spark in his soul, and stubbornly pried open the fist that sought to smother him and his ambitions. He had lived a sheltered life, and longed to reverse the patterns that for so long held him prisoner... the taste of the outside world was no longer fresh inside his mouth.

"I want to swim bare in mother ocean's placental waters," he said to himself, "I want to feel the thorny reefs and behold the colors of the coral. I want to dance in the shadows of the Serengeti, in the manner of the shamans that beckon the rains to drift their way. I want to delve into caves and drift across deserts... laying my feet where oceans have died. Then and only then, can I die happy."

So in dodging the reaper's scythe he set out to see the world the way no dying man was intended to see it... alive with promise and warm-blooded renewal. He hunted the lucent bays in the brotherhood of dolphins, sampling the textures of the coral and counting their vibrant colors. He climbed the snowy peaks and held the brisk mountain air in his lungs, then spent nights in a cavern aglow with quartz and opal. He trudged through the silky dunes as his own beast of burden, where the ghosts of fallen cities haunted the grainy desert winds, and he danced in the African wilderness with the likes of shamans and sorcerers. His body was salted with the seas of the Earth, his pores cleansed with the mountain air, his skin crimsoned by the desert sun. In time he arrived back home, exhausted but strangely unfulfilled.

Then he beheld a beautiful young woman, with eyes of a baffling hue. She glided past him like a robed apparition, oblivious to his presence as she carried herself through the bothers of her day. He thanked the world for her beauty, and felt a comforting sense of awe and satisfaction upon seeing her walk away from his aging eyes. With a subordinate sigh he said at last, "Now I can die with absolution, having finally seen the queen of all corporeal wonders." He returned to the cold sheets of his death-bed, dizzied by the trailing scent of matronly perfume.

But sleep as death would have it still did not come to the man... a new desire tugged at his sleeve and interrupted his concluding thoughts. He sat up suddenly as a newborn vigilance forced open his eyelids... he knew at once what he must do. "I must find the woman of dreams that I saw with my own eyes step across the worldly realm, and make her fall in love with me... then and only then, can I die happy."

The Waiting of the Widow

Manifest a beauty's bane and call her love's nonentity
Embittered muse awaiting her ill husband's waning trinity
Anointed heiress plotting whilst the caregivers attend in herds
Bedside prayers will not find her tidings midst their humbled words

Golden thread of mourning dress; hanging in foreseen pretense
Rose petals in bath water cover she whose heart is dense
Preparing for those whispered words, ceremony cultivates
Sadness from her heart is purged; a joyful greed soon infiltrates

With eyes as dry as desert siftings, she will hide beneath her veil
Not a single tear will stripe her cheek… even as the coffin sails
She coughs into her jeweled hands to blanket an offensive smirk
Taking stock in cautious lies to make her smokescreen magic work

Retiring into empress frill, the funeral just an interlude
Sucking grapes in paradise while fanned by voiceless servitude
She now reclines by fountain side; corruptive sole inheritance
The self-fulfilling prophecy of widow-harvest decadence

Even as her supple skin will gradually depreciate
She still suppresses guilt within, with preconceived success to date
All luxuries accounted for; all paintings, properties and busts
Guards relinquished to her care, once faithful to her husband's trust

"She surely must have loved him, no?" the passersby will say with grief
Every time the manor looms in shadows like a bas-relief
The misconception lingers even as her ballroom brims in May
History will know her as the widow living by the bay

Nescience

A woman was strolling through the woods when she saw a young rose, budding anew and alone on a bush that had not yet fully engulfed its surroundings. She deemed the rose beautiful and flush enough to be picked, so she smiled and kneeled at the edge of the shadows to pluck it from the ground. Before her fingers could gently wrap around the stem, a demon came out of the darkness beyond with a plump rose of much deeper hue in his claws. "Do not waste your want on that feeble rose, my dear," the demon said... "'tis not ripe, but instead a trite and simple bauble that has not been long and will not be much longer. It is a spore of the material world, admired by the fools that dwell in the realm of light. Take my rose in its place, for it is far superior."

The woman, now curious, asked the demon, "Where doth *your* rose come from?"

The demon said, "My rose comes from the ages, from the swirling cosmos and the steaming seas... It is made of the oldest stars and the oldest stone, the farthest moons and the deepest voids. It has been here before the beginning, and will be here long after the end."

But the demon's rose also carried the woes of time, the weight of knowledge, and the foresight of man's doom. The woman looked closer, and in his rose she saw the apple bite and the serpent's bargain, a brother's betrayal and the fall of a great tower. She saw dead cities and ravaged villages, dizzying rows of tombstones and volcanoes spouting ash and flame. So the woman refused the demon's offer, choosing the meeker rose; the rose which was pure, which had only seen the dawn and not yet the ways of man. With it she continued joyfully on... blissfully unaware of the vices of both past and future, forever unspoiled by time and the demon that argued its case.

Sentimental Circles

When I die, my ghost will haunt the cathedral halls and castle tiers of England, Rome and Ireland... lurking between the silence and the echoes in a sanctuary tended to by shuffling monks and housekeepers oblivious to my presence. My spirit will be one with the misty rays that pierce through stained-glass windows glossed with autumn dew, breathing life into their ornate patterns; geometric wonders generously illuminated until the fall of day, reminding one of sunlit dew glinting through an early morning spider web. Even now those grandfatherly structures ferment in preparation for my arrival... and when my eyes find darkness in the peace of night, quantum fluctuations in the pith of my iris begin to color an insightful preview.

Images of holy water cooling under cultured ferns soothe the wounds where earthly attachments have recently been removed, as I walk between the titan doors and into the chapel of calmly whispered prayers. Stair steps frame the room like pyramidal invites, lined with slender candles that light the path for those who come to kneel with floral offerings and dignified pleas for guidance. A dusty organ basks in the valorous light of a chapel window, reaching up to where the less invasive cobwebs are seldom disturbed. Its gilded pipes gleam in the dust-sparkled light like a sculpture poised in triumph, a centerpiece for choral arrangements held only in spirit since silence prevailed as the favorable sermon.

Outside, dustless winds stroke the fields of tall grass like a Greek god running fingers through his golden hair; gently rocking ravens that perch on reeds in a solemn sideways stance. A courtyard nostalgically tinged by autumn's first advancements welcomes ghostly congregations to a podium where weddings are conducted... the kind of weddings that welcome rain at the opportune moment. A wooden carriage idles in see-saw position under a smoky sky, burdened by a spillage of pumpkins and squash that crowds about its mighty wheels. Brittle vines crinkled around a trellis slightly tilted in the soil give off subtle scents of memorable Novembers, mixing with the aromas of hickory smoke and hay stuffed where owls roost.

When the lush of spring embellishes the courtyards and multi-leveled gardens left to cultivate in peace, my ghost will again pass through to inspect the changes nature has reintroduced. A saturated butterfly hangs from a pupa now deflated, drying in rays pied by the branches of graveyard oaks that splash all surroundings with blotches of shade. A bedding of pennies shimmers from the depths of a wishing pond, basking the poolside gargoyles in the unique luster of copper sheen piercing through a varnish of algae. The undercarriage of an overhanging chandelier flickers in the dancing green light, a makeshift strobe that teases the eye in a place of still things.

The stealthy paths of creeks muttering in the shade lead to canals of boat-yielding girth, luring me through quiet hamlets likened to straw roofs and gas lantern windows. Lights of the taverns dance hypnotically in the river below, where the waters project sunset miasmas smeared only by passing mallards who weave through the convex bridges of stone. Though my feet no longer touch the ground, I humor the purpose of stepping stone sidewalks as I sew a path through miles of reeds blackened by the sinking sun... to a crossroads where hutches give way to buildings, and quaint steeples arise to misted clock towers.

Receding storms pigment the clouds over towns where every street is a carnival for the senses... where the fumes of windowsill confections circulate through every alley nook, and the chimneys of bakeries and bread shops exhale cinnamon perfumes into a salmon-colored sky. Train tracks long bereft of wheels sleep under encroaching brush, while the treads of nostalgic automobiles slice through puddles tinted with lukewarm watercolors. Finches scrounge at the legs of apple carts and vendor wagons, their simplistic chirps echoing from curb to curb in an unforgettably familiar fashion. This is the world as told to me by my hopeful eyes, which strain to see beyond the walls of death and into guarded courts.

I will not sever completely from the scenes that I stalked in life, but I will carve new circles of habit out of the places I've wished to be... sampling the Earth's many auras without so much as flinching at vexing distances. As a drifter I will harvest every image that pleases my mind and summon the particles of scattered locales to unite before my own astoundment... with hummingbird visitations I will move through the orchids of a phantasmal display, filling my vials with the antigens of gratifying eidola. These circles are tread with the warm steps of a youth revisited... these circles are tread with intentions to stay.

The Wolves of Bathroe

Solstice, equinox and eve
Now times for holy men to grieve
Evening fumes of hours ill
This night provokes unholy will

Bathroe stirring in the east
Foretelling the end-season feast
A land of shadows splits its gate
To jeopardize who, naked, wait

Smuggled in by legend's care
Averting to the cautious mare
Chilling moan of howls near
Waft into the village ear

Royal pets that hell hath made
With matted hair that masters braid
Each beast an icon to abhor
Armored with malign decor

Demonic messengers athirst
Collecting collars of the cursed
A chase besets a forest run
A dead end makes the circle one

Tooth and talon poison-tipped
Nuzzle carcass maggot-stripped
How acrid steams the freshly killed
Eyes still wide with fear instilled

Wolves of Bathroe haul their feast
To store in wilderness deceased
Gnawing masks the victim's hush
Hidden in the dismal brush

Morning's rescue comes not soon
The sun reveals residual doom
Late, the hour to reconcile
Chiseled skulls to sleep in piles

Mare Clausum

They say I am in love with love, they say I am angry with hate itself... despite my distaste for a critic's accusations, over time I've found that nothing could be closer to the truth. *What a charming way to put it,* I came to think, *to summarize my aesthetic affairs.* Like sailing alone on a private sea I roam freely in a world emptied of nearly everything except for passion; passion in its purest form, exhumed directly from the source without mediators to dilute it in transition. People in my life other than those of mingled blood are now seen as intruders, bent on taking me in a direction I do not wish to go. Their gifts come tainted with a price, and I refuse to pay that price as long as I can feel with my own heart.

I have learned the piper's tune, doing unto others as they've done unto me... Relationships go stale when given the time, and I have too often been a victim of the worldly and their fleeting passions. Now I avoid investing time in building onerous ties, searching for the girl who falls in love with strangers and gives me her heart by the close of day. It is true, I have given up devotion to a taxing pursuit in exchange for an equally exhaustive search... but the irony does not sicken me as one would have me believe.

I still huddle close to misanthropic ideals, and though I do not hate a neighboring soul I do not wish to see his face in the evening. I have what I need to be human, even without the flesh of another... It means more to me than the wrath of unanswered prurience that I should remain aloof in the binds of self-preservation, offering myself unto the altar of misery with the intention of slashing the bridges that cling to past affiliates. Annexed siblings merely carry the illnesses I wish to leave behind, for they will not accept the emerging truth... that you don't need a woman to be a great lover, and you don't need an enemy to be full of hate.

Court of Eons Passed

The past has knowledge the future does not, but whispers its secrets only to the most passionate listeners who refuse to let the future waft them away. Nature progresses in form to the tune of voices sparring in the halls of mass perception... Visionary men retelling the world's birth since the age of undiscovered truth, narrating but one stride in the endless dance of the mind and heart. For them, Earth's past is up for grabs... and it is any fool's guess as to what masterly force piloted our ascension from the sea.

What cycles flourished beyond the walls of Eden that we might speculate so carelessly in the pages of so many dissonant tomes? The stubborn dreamer imagines great cities of gold skewed by winish rivers running red with potions of desire, all forbidden to the senses of mortals. One might envision gluttonous serpents coiled around the Greek columns of the pavilion, spilling about the marble steps while fruit-fed heathens stroke and fan them in the shadow of truculent deities.

Let not your mind be honeyed with such outrageous imagery... 'Tis nothing but a sugar cube for the liar's tongue, and you'd be better off leaving it for some tribal primitivist to swallow. For instead of the golden redolence of kingdoms having long slept, we find in the soil the awkward bones of beasts unwritten... preserved in baffling death throes that will surely mislead the envisioning naturalist. We also find the missing subterranean volumes of fragmentary literature, awakening radical new perspectives on once tolerated scriptures.

The probing tendrils of science have fondled only the shallowest of fossil beds; many peculiar things never see the light of day, save for those relics regurgitated by the restlessness of the Earth. Empires, too, have fallen under the mercy of the plates; natural disasters make their contributions to the cruel advancements of time, leaving precious belongings reclaimed by a volcanic tragedy to sleep under grey seas of ash. Learned men will take the stand to justify the uncovering of these curiosities, calling out ancient sesquipedalian texts as evidence as they bleed forgotten troughs once sealed in the name of quieting blasphemy. Aftermath is a resilient stain, for even dead cities are not easily forgotten.

Aged paintings drooping on museum walls remember even plagues and battles lost, the breath of their stories synchronized with the yellowing of pages whose edges have been singed by time. The more pressing artifacts found only a fate in bonfire cinders... submitted in flame to immobilize some exotic fever. They had not a chance to travel far from their home... those lonely islands cleared of life, left only with the wreckage of disease... where scavenging spirits stalk the tell-tale bone yards, voiceless banshees midst the fumes of heat-scorched skeletons long stripped of carrion. Only a witchdoctor's jewels have immunized to the flames, sifted out of the ash by some black market peddler and sent to the scrutiny of an unlawful master. Evidence, you see, may travel many hands before it is offered to the jury of modern day sentience.

Mountains birth in the oceans where visibility descends in hue, and great trenches swallow creatures glittering in the deep… volcanoes pass in and out of slumber, and trees sprout from the ashes of forests surrendered to a greater cause. As tides are leveled and cocoons are split, leaves turn and glaciers shift, the resilience of timeless riddles left by these episodes becomes increasingly hard to ignore… sculpting secrets at the edge of impressionable ears as the devil on Darwin's shoulder. The present will continue to prosecute the past, courtroom philosophers ablaze with conflict. Answers retract from the edge of light, refusing to enlighten the harbingers of legend.

Needless to Say

Needless to say, Mr. Aberdeen, I won't be courting your lovely daughter… I have made amends with a just maiden more worthy of my heart's bias. Even now she waits for me among the rustic shadows of home, faithfully waiting to reunite with my fireside presence so that she may listen to tales anticipated through lonely winters passed. Do not find stringency in my words… I do not wish to deny the merit of your offer… but faith is a thing that must be rewarded in order for karma to make its journey beyond the moral failures of a previous life. She trusts me as the mare trusts its rider of three years or more, and I shall not be the devil to break the bond that has kept our love afloat.

Truly your daughter is a force of beauty, and I would be a fool to refuse her hand as it reaches to be ringed… but that fool I must claim to be, for the beauty I call my own is a kind native to the land that waits for me so many backward miles over the sea. There my maiden stands with a pail of water weighting each hand, in a tattered dress that speaks subtly of rural demands and smells of autumn chimneys stifled with boiling broth. Her eyes are as brown as dampened timber, her hair as black as crumbled coals; the raspy sough of her buxom voice as commonplace as the call of a crow. Thistles and burs cling to her flowing locks, barbed wire scratches glisten on her calves… all telling tales of her disdain for boundaries that struggle to keep trespassers at bay. For her, they are mere hurdles on the path to twilight prairies bronzed by a deepening sun.

Needless to say, Mr. Aberdeen, I am spoken for should the matter arise. No vixen of the new world could outshine my rustic queen, or keep me long from the homeland that knew our lives combined. I yearn to find her waiting there, perhaps daydreaming in the arms of an oak, or peering coyly from the edge of an old barn door… our fireside tales will then resume, when this wayside errand releases me back to her arms.

Clear My Conscience

You are the holy water that steams at my waist
As I submerge 'til it singes my face

You are the rose petals that fall from the sky
Collecting at my feet as I doubt my own eyes

You are the stake that rusts in my heart
Keeping my arousals a century apart

You are the cross at the head of my bed
Delaying my demons while prayers are said

You are the Nile that sours into blood
Taunted by pharaohs on the riverbed mud

You are the wafer I don't want to swallow
Red wine dissolves where my stomach is hollow

You cleanse me; I don't see the point in your toil
When death claims me, I'll just return to the soil
Still I allow you to pluck out my sins
Wiping my eyes clean of tears never been

My dear, clear my conscience but I will refrain
The wild in the animal you'll never tame
I am the raven and you are the dove
That is the flux of our forbidden love

So it is Written

Holiness shines before the bewildered eyes of peasantry, as the face of a healer is groped by tenacious hopefuls; ailing souls that fall about his feet and tug at his robe with their needful pleas unnumbered. In the banquet hall, flies descend upon the heretics' feast, and poison settles at the bottom of their glasses... waiting to be swallowed by those selected for damnation. This balance sustains itself with a reflex of cruelty, as these legendary processes build upon the strata of our souls. Even as creation rises and falls in divinity's open palm, we will never stray far from the garden where our plague began... we will never shake the vines that grapple our ankles on our quest to escape inadequacy.

Typecast by our bodies, fenced in by our flaws, we are actors enlisted in a spectacle we cannot turn away from. We are gears entranced by the mechanics of apathy, engaged in the rabid fairy-ring of life as a link within a chain of imps. The relief of reincarnation denied; the soul, no matter how seasoned, is diverted back into the original strain to honor a primitive codex. No man or woman may find refuge in another form, and if saints were to teach them well they would warn against investing faith in higher levels of being.

What pity that a heart is a prison for a soul, and a brain is a prison for a mind... and what bathos that mankind should fall short of divinity, instead confined to an exchange of daggers and spears. The fabric of flesh tears so easily under the dragging of a blade... how dare it be assigned to guard the livelihood of a soul's spark! Worse yet, even upon exceeding mortality the spirit cannot disband its lifelong label, for the confines of gender and the weight of memory survive to restrict our walks in heaven.

The shepherd's hands outstretch to caress the bleating snouts of his goats and lambs, as they lick his fingers clean of residual grain with a fervor attributed to those condemned to a life of desire. Communion with beasts only strengthens the division of breeds... between fates god-chosen and fate self-imposed. Still the banquet halls of heathens bustle with reckless shadows... serpents flicking their tongues across the hot nape of night, reveling in a jungle of treasures never meant to feel the sweat of a mortal's palms. Ignorance to the price of longing seems to free us from angelic responsibilities, and if there is no escape from the roles we've been assigned then there is no more sense in forgetting the language of the flesh.

The Storm Herald

When prophecy stains the skies, a solitary figure in black reaches out to the gathering storms… 'Tis a dark priest well versed in devilry; a man who has the power to bring instantaneous damnation upon himself with the utterance of a single word. With defiant spells thrown from a seaside ledge, his intention is to hit like that first shuddering of thunder… speaking in a voice that cannot be ignored. Feared is a wizard who can conjure hail and funnel clouds from the white of his palms, and had the locals recognized him beyond his peasant garb they would have halted him before he reached that cliff and spread his arms. Now, a rising king in his own mind, he summons the winds to blow through his wintry hair and rustle the manes of the Apocalypse horses… Thunder marks the birth of powerful things, and light cowers when its forces are outnumbered.

Spirits awaken from vortices unseen, called to their war drums as th conductor raises his wand in preparation for the percussive symphony. Thunderheads ooze in from a silver-sheen horizon, bringing with them the midnight drapery that smothers the landscape… extinguishing the odd shades of light that preceded the approaching cataclysm. That deceptively ornate sky was an oracle for unwelcome events, and now it retires under the weight of clouds that pulse with a proliferating ink. Gates to troubled realms are thrust wide open, allowing the imbalance of Armageddon to blanket the fields with tumors of shade.

Seaside cottages seal their shutters to sever from the distressing sight, leaving restless clotheslines to spiral with abandoned garments. Veins of lightning spear the horizon, paling the purple sky to reveal the last remnants of avian life fleeing for shelter… led by their instincts on wings that struggle to maintain pace against conflicting winds. In time the spell is in play, and a mock end of days has the coastline sealed in a coffin of death-fearing panic. Waves hurl themselves at the shore, shattering in an epic cymbal crash of destructive influence. Shards of white foam pierce the rain in a fractious cross-current, sending airborne ripples through a homogenous mix of saltwater and storm perspiration. The reach of fearless tides is exceeded only by the crawling clouds that bubble forth like boiling blisters of tar, souring the newly envious spirits of the sea with gaudy crests of their own.

The chanting children of a black-robed cult, unflinching against the tidal spray, stand like drones along the jagged rocks only yards from where the gleaming stones surrender to the ocean's rage. When their song is done they drop into the black, swallowed by storm-teased waves that play their part with ritual concordance. The naïve probing of a lighthouse reveals no trace of their having entered the surf, for they are well on their way into the dissolution of sacrifices swallowed… where the very phosphorescence of the living deep is smothered under a veneer of onyx waves. Mainlanders mourn not for minions of rituals woven to dark passages read by somber voices; their destiny runs askew to that of casualties fallen under black skies. After all, demons and their slaves should not trouble absorbents of the sun with their necrotic devotions.

Is it any wonder that witnesses to this barbituric display fear for the well-being of the world's natural order? Clouds so burdensome to the sky, winds as fickle as a sinner's soul... these elemental agents gone awry give no pity to the suffocation of God's splendor, and surely the final judgment will rise from an ocean troubled as this. Until the lone figure on the crag lowers his hands and closes his cloak, the abodes of surface-dwellers will bear witness to glimpses of a time not far from life's keel... a time when the serpent will no longer crawl, but will regain influential forms unwholesome to the faulty will of man and womankind. Misfortune spills over the dam once upheld by heroic remembrance, and ill tidings spawn in the currents of turbulent tides unclean.

You Are Joy

Further down the wandering path
I recollect what time-lords hath…
Encrypted as our curious tale
Me, blood-red, and you so pale

Your childlike smile, my broken heart
Each of them will play their part
The darkness of my life will prove
That you are needed there to soothe

Seems I left you in a stream
Of tears and woes and damsel screams
Still I know your virgin slate
Destroying while you recreate

Hand in hand, we walk the mile
With you I will reconcile
I am minus to your plus
You are faith in both of us

Your sun will shine on strong 'til noon
Before abating into gloom
The gloom that turned my heart to stone
But I will never be alone

I'm the grasp of day gone dim
That wraps around your fragile stem
I am master, you are toy
I am sadness, you are joy

Lentissimo

Have you ever felt that heavy feeling… the feeling that compares your minimal being to a presence of great density?

Like the marriage of majesty and mass… When there are cellos playing in your heart, and the weight of the ocean heaves against your chest.

The feeling that brings you shipside to observe great churning oars dragging the oily waters in an oafish cadence…

And massive black waves in a lentissimo state of physical hypnosis; a vision that must have aided many composers in the metering of their darker symphonies.

What shadows lurk in the bulk of the soul, so that men may concoct these opiate arrangements merely at the sound of the rain or sea?

Make no mistake that murky paintings and severed statues spawn from the same cloud…

…For they all dress the demons otherwise left naked in the oils of the subconscious.

In Weeping for Lost Bibelots

The great lizard will sleep and he will dream the key to the cosmic gate, thereby purging the flooded caverns of time so that those who search for precious things may filter the most impossible spaces. A celestial crossroads with dimensional travelers haunting every vertex will open its many mouths, venting hidden nights whose stars obey only ancient patterns. Ringed planets pebble an ebony atrium sparked by meandering meteor glimpses, all pieces in an intricate mobile that dangles over desert dusk. Stair-step valleys brim with flowering cactus columns taller than suggested by sanity, and moon-dust mesas raise their secrets from the grasp of devouring sands.

The clout of heavenly bodies wills clouds and winds into a fateful orbit, past cooling dunes purpled by the setting sun… into a marketplace still concealed by ripples of heat, where the chimes of foreign percussion and the croaking of hogs and hens are the dialects of choice. Beings of curious trade mingle with the wind-rippled tents, but the objects sought are not among their colorful quarries. Nomads quest between oases, dragging their debts across viscous seas of sand to reach patient ships resting faithfully at ocean's edge… from there the voyages peak into feverish battles with sailors' woes, as sirens shriek lest men reach the lavishly gardened Zion of a deity's hybrid brethren.

There, nourishing forces birth new concepts… like a lush courtyard peopled by albino pheasants scattering to avoid the strides of a beastly caravan, upon which a childlike emperor of indeterminable age rides atop a satin pillow. Servants follow with gifts on their shoulders, but none of these things are the treasures whispered of in a tale's beginnings. On the far side of the valley a palace gleams of a mineral no longer found elsewhere, catching the light in mysterious ways. Inside paces a king shadowed by a most peculiar curse… to be immortal and still be plagued by fears of death, until the grace of a wizard releases him from his debts.

Even farther lies the county of willing exiles, where runoff from the mountains brings trace amounts of Olympian residue to the villages below. Tales said that warriors who came from that land had swords made of diamond, and they used them tenaciously and without hesitation… as though they feared not for dirtying them or losing them in battle. Shopkeepers with strange birds on their shoulders peer from behind veils of white hair, their eyes glimmering with a hint of royalty in disguise. Behind them stare wooden shelves stuffed with banded scrolls, tinted jars and books with bindings reduced to thread… but the ultimate object of desire has already been purchased and carried off on the back of some bard long gone.

There is a madman that sleeps by the rain barrel outside the tavern; his fragmented tales tell of glorious lost things and of longing and yearning... and of returning pilfered pieces to their rightful home with a reluctance to depart with their wonderment despite a need to restore order. Behind his frenzied gaze there seems to stir a deeper knowledge, one that healthier men might covet should they know its true caliber... but steady yourself at your limits, my friend, for you never know the price he paid for that knowledge. Fools only retract when burned by the ills of obsession, and acrid is the grievance for artifacts that did not survive the transition from dream to reality...

The Hole

I shan't forget that horrendous yawning sound; the chorus of a billion ailing ghosts caught in slow-churning vortex, which in truth became the wail of cosmic winds circling up through unmanageable depths... Nor will I forget the infinite darkness that stole from my soul as I gazed into it hopelessly and without deviation. The afterlife speaks bitterly of such dour caverns that our spirits, even without their timid shells, approach with wary dwarfishness. God forbid I should transcend that crater's edge and tumble down the chute of the damned, doomed to fare the true meaning of oblivion... I might never again feel the blessing of solid ground, but rather bathe in accursed inertia until I rot in the very state of falling. That would be the hour that sold me to the pythonic wonders of subterranean night... where even the unreceptive Ithaqua stops us at the edge and inquires, "Foolish mortal, what business brings you here?"

Autumn in Babylon

When the seasons speak their fickle words
And the sky is dark with southbound birds,
Kingly feasts go under knife
In exotic courtyards livid with life

Liquid arcs from fountains gray
Cherubs dancing in water play
Centerpieces for circular paths
These cherub fountains and pebbled baths

Coffee-tint horses with ivy for stirrups
Carry twin pails of absinthian syrup
Animals harnessed all bring to the feast
Dark wines and dark breads, to speak of the least

Tables of marble where fruit quarries spill
A tanager leaves with a grape in its bill
One loftily perched gazes curiously down
Eyeing the grapes on a senator's crown

Warrior-philosophers gorge in repose
Laughing, their faces aglow like the rose
Splashes of cherry ale carelessly spilt
From gold-handled cups as they joyously tilt

Twilit pavilions where stargazers meet
Bustling about at a statue's gray feet
Moving through counters of quill-pens and globes
Leaf-littered floors trawled by Babylon robes

Stone columns painted by flickering fires
Leaf-burning beacons twixt Babylon spires
Daylight withdraws its flaxen-curl breath
Retiring summer with slight ease of death

An arsonist sunset ignites the field brush
For paradise flowers soon wilt as they blush
So odd that the hour of autumn has chimed
In a paradise city still hidden from time

I Among Others

I dare to come forward as a representative of a troubled race, even though my bond with others of my kind has not been duly confirmed. Whether or not other tribes share in my particular crop of ailments is a mystery yet to be dissolved, however I trust that a common ancestor is not too far out of focus. Mortals in limbo, a typical sight for angels restrained from coming to aid, will always crater this desperate Earth... forever bound to its heretic cycle as the key holders to a most baneful mass memory. With salted wounds and chains to drag, my fellow man sickens down to his ribs with a spiritual famine more hollowing than the locust cloud... I kneel helplessly and do nothing, for I too breathed of the virus that unifies our damnation.

Our inherent obsession, to find restitution in a place undefined; our guiding light, the volatile mixture of failure and ambition. Is it a naïve assumption to think we should find answers after death? Will we be forced to forget such riddles in compliance with life's retreat? Questions unanswered tinge our torch to carry, yet still we hoist the burden as we distribute it amongst faith's dwindling beacons. We with noble hearts want nothing more than to know that innocence does not exist in vain and the price of compassion will profit in the end... but premonitions of peace gasp in the stiffening coils of jeopardy, while honor frantically weighs the unmediated debts of human exchange.

A pallbearer of our misguided breed blindly gropes his chosen way... carrying with him a mistrust of the senses, burdened by the book of cynical process. Another of our kind delves headfirst into any vat of water that gleams of purported holiness, ignoring the greenish tinge that hints of heathen grade. But no matter what corner of the spectrum my cellmates choose to gravitate towards, the mortal desperation that oozes out of the clenched fist of the gods will luster with my blood as well as theirs, for my veins brim with both flavors of erroneous design. We are siblings on a banished ship cursed with strains of plague... the jaded disciple, the unhallowed priest, and he who kneels in naivety... all doomed to sink like a sea bound pyre having exhumed its last drifting ember.

Perhaps I have too long paled my vision through a pessimist's monochrome eyes, ignoring the auroras of hope that glimmer even now in the milk of the horizon. So often existence translates into pain, but as sure as there is a burning blade there is a sheath to cool it. It is true that it is unlikely for miracles to reveal themselves, but this does not mean they do not stir beneath our notice... I have failed to calculate these subliminal miracles each time I paused to assess life's offerings, for they fit so well into my meshed surroundings that my eyes refused to detect them. Now I see that my species is as much likened to a race of initiators as it is a race of failures, and despite the chains piled at our feet we will learn to drag them to new slopes of self-discovery. Together we will make use of the obscured tools at our disposal and awaken talents unrealized, shaping faith as it shapes us in turn... Our vices are only there to keep us from competing with the arrogance of divinity, and our limitations are merely there to ease us into molds of self-restraint.

Canaan

It is a golden age when the achievements of civilizations once opposed allow them to advance in harmony... when energy is harvested from a wisp of the air and war is dispelled through the distractions of technological marvels rather than the implementation of them. It is a turning point, a pivotal era... when Zen beings from other planets study Earth's life forms through painless and constructive methods. Life is lengthened to unimaginable degrees, and those already long deceased now reenter the world through scientific miracles that transcend the horrors of genetics. In the midst of it all, a man in complete awe of his own species' capabilities... his fear of life having long gone the way of cancer's extinction, replaced by a bewilderment likened to a child first exposed to the light.

It seemed like only seconds ago in the universe's saga that men were merely cells mingling beneath the ocean's facade, gelled by some blindly amorous prototype of will. Now they erect great towers that babble code into the depths of infinity, nestled against the cosmos with open ears. Enter the race that heard music in the breath of stars and dark bodies alike... the race that harnessed the furtive resources of seemingly desolate worlds in orbit; resources unappreciated by the soulless galaxies that seethed and swelled around them.

The secrets of death and life have been awarded to those newly knighted for their tact, and the original creator remains unoffended by the accomplishments of his children. A truce between science and religion unlocks discoveries that could shake any skeptic off his perch, while the makings of a tangible heaven on Earth percolate under a sun saved from impending fatigue. Never again will man separate himself from the outer realms in fear, nor will he dismiss journeys to his most distant neighbors as a romance out of reason. Never again will he battle over documents valued for deadly designs, nor will he strike his brother down to harvest land that neither one calls home. Museums alone tell the hardships of the past, curated by white-robed monks that ensure the longevity of the sun. It is a dawn where infinity is at last embraced, and peace begins life as an undisputed reality.

Heir to Enigma

Enigma has the better part of me wrapped around its finger; I exhaust every day writhing at the point of its ungula, pinned without volition to escape. The offerings of this existence are disheveled curiosa, its words an epitaph left to puzzle onlookers who caress its chiseled words. Questioning the practices of nature is a symptom of our forefathers, one that we will not so deftly leave behind when we crawl from the nest.

Why is the night so musical and the day so modestly ambient? The answer, of course, is that the wings of things that thrive in the night are not like the wings of things that thrive in the day... still my curiosity is not set with the tale. Why is pleasure so illusory and sadness so readily made? It seems that sadness is a simple recipe while happiness requires ingredients scarce to be found. Even so, why does sorrow cling to the winter while spring finds lovers at their peak? Such questions course through my veins like a lingering venom, and my curiosity... like an unwanted immortality... may never be quelled to sleep.

Do I truly care, or am I afraid of guilt? Do I truly love, or am I afraid of being alone? These shameful thoughts and vices, do they speak the truth of me... or are they mere appendages cultivated by the proceedings of malignance? Furtive spirits whisper to each other as I pass in daily paces, but I cannot hear what they are saying... only the crossroads of death will reveal the verdict they have chosen, and then I will know whether to bear stigma or to kneel under the alighting sword of redemption. Do the heavens brag of me, or do they pity my blindness? Am I a martyr for peace, or a martyr for devils? I have carried defiance in my chalice for many miles, though I drink with hesitation in discord for its bitter taste. What, in truth, does this say of my nature?

The great beyond withholds its secrets from those who refuse to surrender themselves to oblivion. In light of this, must every man ail from a fascination with death that is coupled with a reluctant fear? And, in clone fashion, must every man defy initial wisdoms and suffer from a mass rejection of erudite functionality? Although there are many riddles I still refuse to release from my grasp, I can share with you this one proverb I have stumbled upon thus far... A man may only learn of himself what he dares to chase into his soul, and he will only reap from nature what he will accept in its rightful form.

A Thousand Ways

A simple joy to soak the wound, the only thing the pain obeys
To picture a most pleasant moment, and picture it a thousand ways
Interbreeding memories and reinventing wishful vows
Contemplating altered outcomes, every form my mind allows

The only way for time to pass when suff'ring designated tasks
To lie in bed, desires vexing; entertained by riddles sexing
Musings hollowed through and through; there's nothing left to do but to…
Admit defeat to lofty gods, and pray for pleasure when distraught

Amygdala

Those faithful to the future place no value on the perception that my allies and I possess; my correspondence with the past will always be ridiculed by the usual devotees of logic. They attest that my tongue is trained only for the confection of denial and not for the bitter ale that has strengthened the bones of my ancestors. I vainly attempt to repel that stigma through the fickle voice of doubt, for I have kept an eggshell piece of those dim days when the song of motherhood kept my cradle in motion. When you crack the fist that is my daily defense you will see that I am but a child in its palm, orphaned by my own life as it rushes ahead of me.

Déjà Vu is an old friend, reaching out to cushion my side with a familiar sense of reassurance… a feeling that somehow always seems to find its way back to my doorstep in spite of time's intentions. An old song nests in an old day… a droning nostalgia weighs me down into sedative sleep, and I would be foolish to resist even had I somehow grown suspicious of unsettling news lurking ahead. As my head clouds with incited remembrance, I take liberties and rummage through life's pictorial array… cerebral snapshots having survived the chasmic leaps of unidirectional rubric; the porches and power-lines of a mawkish memorandum. Backtracking to that rustic place will never seem a wasted effort, and I deepen the path each time with a greater sense of purpose.

The choral voices of past acquaintances sing to me life's more subtle lessons, reminding me of the formula that I swore by long before stigma singed my skin… a pulse assuring me that I still carry the sweet ache of memory within my chest, an anchor I never tire of. Those places formed the pool from which I rose… sentimental sites bereft of the privilege to revisit them, or to even recall them at all. Even the ones that escape my grasp must be listed to my credit, lest my army of resilient qualities be excluded from my timeline's very fibers. I wish to speak for even the most minute of experiences, no matter how meek they may be in the shadow of mental landmarks.

The weary faces of the newly dead, stooped over the Lethe with a reluctance waning in light of their thirst, know the threat that those waters reflect… I, too, risk a curse to bewail my prime; to mourn the welfare of the mist-tinseled infancy whose hymns to remind are gradually giving way to silent failure. I will not be so quick to release my belongings into the abyss, and I will have every waking moment etched into my soul before I join my forefathers in their sleeping cells between the stars. A maniacal stubbornness, innate and undying, keeps me prodding the coals well into the night, as to keep the fire alive for many more a song to its end.

With a venerable defiance gilded with infantile sentiments, I will again wet the canvas with the colors of even the dimmest dawn, be it rescued from the amnesic plunge and restored to life from the darkest catacombs of youth overstepped. True, the improved cutlery of a new day's misery waits for me with blades exposed, but even tomorrow I will deny mortality's nagging reminders that life is a solvent unto flesh. No matter how deftly pain evolves to match my steps and force me into forward motion, I must allow joy some room for respiratory ease… tending to sacred flames not yet surrendered to ash. I will never waive my right to gaze once more into the wild eyes of youth, before turning away and forgetting her beautiful face at last.

Mirror Envy

Buried between the pages of life's early chapters, a darkness that pulses with bigeminal heartbeats. Cradled beside me in the void, the brother I never had... given form by way of imagination, given life by way of blind creation. He would be the one to resurrect me at the edge of my potential, challenging me and mentoring me in one primal stride. He would be a warrior... equal parts vicious and noble... like the wolf that captures so much awe. A seizure of the Earth awakens a spore in the depths of possibility, a seedling of my psyche that ruptures molds of both devil and god... only to withdraw back into laughable dreams and leave me to brave life's beatings alone.

His eye, though warmly alive, would have overtones of sly apathy reminiscent of the serpent's vertical slice... but in that same eye would swim the valor of an eagle and the sated conceit of a lion resting in the shade. His expressions, penetrating... his movements, well-crafted... my exalted brother to be would be a raw marvel of nature, supplementing my pacifism with the Dionysian aesthetics required to complete a well-furnished balance. Even when our swords clashed I would not question his existence, for men of Eastern thought have long raved of the necessity of opposing forces. In the end his role would prove to be meaningful, though not without first engaging me in a battle of wits in regard to that meaning.

On some detached astral plane, had I shared a womb with another? Wading through a thick sea of strangers, I long to touch brows with my one true counterpart... to engage in a telepathic bout of blood brother communion. Should revelation incarnate crouch in wait for me among the clouds of a life paralleled, I would accept his intrusion and allow my most innate qualities to reflect back at me with semi-quarrelsome duality. This lonesome and maddening whim, this most intricate need for my soul to stir up an echo, might live to see such an outrageous wish granted and the birth of a welcome antithetic agent rupture. Then, our saga will advance out of the mire of speculation and into the realms of matter and flesh; brothers beyond a contrast in mothers, brothers engaged in an undying circuit.

Invert Your Oars

Join me as I pivot foot
And turn to face where days redeem
Revisiting archaic shores
As if the past were still upstream

We sprint through houses resurrected
Walls that guarded us in youth
Where secrets crouched from summer's light
Darkness knew our voice in truth

From yesterhour to yesteryear,
Laughter turns back into tears
And then we through the pain remembered…
Return twice fold to joys retendered

Coffins open to the morn'
Releasing fellows born again
Newborns into blankets laid
As when they first knew mother's skin

Sidewalk mists of storms long passed
Recollect on fabled streets
Through them we retrace our steps
Again our fates are ours to cheat

From yesterhour to yesteryear,
We gaze back on rekindled fears
Then over previous hurdles course
To find again that braver source

So ne'er query wisemen why
The colors of the forests fade
Or why as wombs are lastly tried,
An elder from a child is made

Instead resolve a silent wish
To cut the brush back from the track
And meet me on the farthest end
Together we will circle back

Tributaries

There is much to be said for the one who falls out of line or out of love… the stray lamb that drifts beyond the shepherd's staff… for he ventured over that uncertain hill and returned to me with stories of sterling intrigue. His claims attest to the reach of the river's arms; the burgeoning hydrae that spill from the frayed ends of a warrior's road and tickle the chin of curiosity with their voltaic fibers. In the cradle of this woven thread lies the glory of lives in question… the pages that wrote my world and yours are now awash with solvent ambiguity, and the frozen cast of fortune thaws to a pool at our feet. The will of the dice to attorn is strong, but the gambits of volatile souls scheme on a much higher plane… The mystery of multiple fates becomes my creed as loose ends are left to dangle in the deflecting currents.

Another romance diverted, another destiny ignored… the unheard death of what could've been, softly laid into its morning grave. For the first time I am confident that life has no writ, and I realize that the cards provide nothing that can't be mutilated through interpretation. Your crystal ball glows with static, mere snapshots of random musing that are no more Delphic than the gibberish a child scrawls on paper. Forgive me for not sanctioning guidance in forms endowed with life, but I am content with the darkened eyes of fate as they have earned no more acuity than that with which they began.

There is no mortal contract that I cannot unfasten, no terrestrial skin that I cannot shed with diligent writhing; with a few well-placed moves I am freed from a choking hold and liberated unto nameless pastures. I choose not to leave my mark on a world that has so rudely left its mark on me… but gaze not in quandary as I take from the gardens of experience without so much as leaving a footprint in the soil, for primary scriptures spoke nothing of my birth and the secondary scriptures will in turn speak nothing of my death. Eons hard fought and far traveled will not so much as utter my next move, and time will soon forget me as it visits grander isles in the spatial oceans of entity. No prophet will boast *my* tale as he prates to his people from a stone tablet, and the sheep that discovered his own source of solace will be the glyph of yet unwritten sagas.

A Pledge to Xenia

Asleep at the ocean's rim, a town between heroes, enjoying the peace before awakenings of war... waiting for a new rogue adventurer to dock its shores and complete his epic tale. It is rare that such chivalry, even be it a fluke, should arrive on needy soil without dragging a net full of ulterior motives. Be that as it may, Viking channels rich with remembered anguish will one day know the path of a less dooming keel; a docile-flagged ship that seeks merely to distance itself from a crippled homeland and escape the soured rulers who cast their web over utopia.

There is a land whose language is owed to past invasions, to the ironic evolution of kingdoms conquered and conquered again. Isthmoid avenues have delivered the influence of settlers eager to renovate, invoking the pollination of worlds apart. The viral nature of religion has sent self-propagating gods and devils into newly parted crevices, swaying heathens to and fro by inducing pagan acts of fear. New laws brought once honorable men to their knees before rising powers, as wars flexed the boundaries between holy ground and unyielding wasteland. Through the smoke of battles passed a residual wisp of knighthood still struggles to prevail, echoing the words of rebel priests that are now exalted as fathers of peace.

It is not uncommon to judge a race of men by how they respect their dead, as well as how they regard the ones who walk beside them in life... by their willingness to cloak the cold stranger who stumbles in from the storm, warming him with their blankets and broth. Xenia, the code by which Greek men had fathered children, rightfully paid for a peddler's apple or carried a pail for a tiring woman... should bring gifts to trade on a galley bound for new land, so that avid pioneers can make peace with the natives and colonize without jealous intent.

It is a far cry from where the islanders still greet ships with their spears held high, stomping out into the shallows to intercept arrivals with an angry zeal. These savages have not yet found the code that humanity has taken centuries to sculpt, instead pruning fires built in the interests of voodoo... readying them for sanguine feasts that begin with the rasp of painted death rattles. Adventurers who stumble upon these lesser lands will not cultivate the love affair standardized by pilgrims and tribesmen, but will find in its place a welcoming of cults and decidedly primal mores. Dream not of beautiful brown-skinned women who come to lay flowers around your neck, but rather impoverished wenches with ghost-eyed children at their side; waiting for virgin blood to suffice for the sustenance of dwindling cattle and crops.

Just as the blood culture of the Mayans reserves no lofty seat for newcomers – save for one on the sacrificial slab – the audacity of primitive societies has been known to resist the evolution of hospitality. Chivalrous doctrines have met their share of friction from the shunned dark corners of the map, and still they find foes in the urbane realms of the mainland, but the purpose of benevolent forces will not become extinct despite the survivals of ancient tribal malice.

Epitaphs chiseled by the starry-eyed entourages of heroes still demand that virtue adapt and leap readily to the call of divine duty… so that men may not wallow in the deep end of their own mortality, or inflict upon their brothers the woes of folkloric tragedy. "Let it be known," imply the grooved letters entrenched beneath a statue's limestone sandals, "that seekers of new land shall not blight it with their exhausting desires and build upon those ashes their intrusive cities… instead they shall settle for the quaint cottages of a humbled society and forfeit the dizzying architectural spectacles enabled by the sweat of slaves." When those words are scribed and taken under arm in journeys afar, the torch of salvation will be freed to pass hands and make its way across outlying margins. Friction between forest and city will fail, and spears and rifles will lower in tandem.

Looking Back, I Love Her

With the passiveness of gray-blue eyes, I let those years slip away... She is now but a wraith at my side, an after image of blushing skin wrapped in winter garments. A woman to parallel my life and mentor me through the maze is no longer a profit of my surroundings, and I look to the waiting wings of destiny with qualms for the ride to come. The pretentious juggling act of starving one drive to feed another has led me to choose between bride and bereavement; what foolishness sent me running to the arms of the latter I cannot name. I left her standing there, flowers drooping in hand, bewildered at my sudden exit... Miles away I carved a new life bereft of wedding white, deaf to church bells and blind to pearls and veils.

If this twist of fate was a mere augmentation of a loaded chessboard, I wonder if the stars approved the move... to outgrow the warmth of love and wander out into the cold rain, a strategy charted by one damnably selfish whim. Like slipping on wet stone I clumsily explored life's outer reaches, sailing on greed's tangents with the vigor of a sailor maddened from his losses on land and his years at sea. Now my only lover is the darkness that exists without her arms, and I saw the clouds approaching though I could not confess to it when euphoric feelings were at their crest.

As for her, she spoke of my endeavors as if she knew they'd take me away... it were as though she possessed some psychic knowledge of my imminent departure. Perhaps she merely kept my lust for independence in sight as it grew, secretly prepared to accept the inevitable with a sigh and a turn of her head. In truth it was her who lost a pillar to stand on; I weep not for the severed root left in *my* garden. My conscience laid out careful instructions for her emotional upbringing... for the care of a delicate woman-child designed for tenderness and not for hardship... but no, I left her to the wolves; turned her loose to the very world we once denied, hands clasped between our bodies in pride.

I stand now at a crossroads, remembering with guilty pain as the wind scrapes my empty hands. The wind smells like closure, and though it speaks to you of fresh rain on the lips of roses it carries for me a pungency I hesitate to inhale deeply. I realize now what merit resonated within that unblemished heart, and I remember her blameless for I was the one to forfeit a precious thing of value for the limited quarry of vagrant life. I dared to take a breath after the fastening of my heart, a mere moment to step back and gauge my feelings for her... but that moment swelled and covetously stole me as its own. That moment... became my life.

Something of a Gem

I weep at your beauty, cringe at your wrath
Unnerved by your stare, relieved at your laugh
I bring you taboos at your every call
My legs in your chains, I stumble and fall

You quiver my kiss, I wince at your hand
I serve at your side with a frond for a fan
Your bed is a coffin of velvets and furs
I fancy your heel has a poisonous spur

A javelin into my heart you incline
On newly slain prey by the fireplace dine
I weep at your beauty, cringe at your wrath
But I shall not choose… an alternate path

A Delayed Affair

You left not a lone widow but rather scores of grieving ascendants; the black drones that wept in rows at your funeral. I was not there, for I would have been a dove in a line of crows… however the day of your death left me pondering in my chamber. I thought of how our little game ended in your disgust, and how my ill-placed remark willed you to override your love of sport and terminate our gestating bond. I could detect the witful ends in the patterns of your pawns, a rousing delegation that will not go unnoticed in the eyes of your newfound clan… the subterranean allegiance has won a whip of a wordsmith, and the mark of your intelligence will topple their kings. With your femme intuition you will charm the dead, even at their moment of initial inspection.

Would I be rabid to say I wish to meet you after death? I was stimulated by your verse even after your passing, and I feel we still have much to converse in the manner of babbling eccentrics. May the wall that shut me out crumble in light of your new situation, may the possibility of romance arise with the mention of eternity. I seem to prefer a woman of ethereal magnitude; what better woman for me than the one who combines immateriality with the wit and vigor I seek in life? Only a woman recently offered unto the realm of death can allow me anticipate an unlikely tryst… I do hope that our conversations will continue despite such grim circumstances.

I trust that you will find new ways to channel your charismatic banter, whispering in the ears of astral travelers while I prose the limited value of earthly things. Perhaps I will tire of my corporeal affairs and seek you out on your own terms, daring to cross the boundaries set by natural forces to enfold your wistful haunting grounds. An epicene aroma will complement your lair, a pansexual aura will coil around your throne and beckon me to yoke with its power. With lily hands unfolding you will tempt me with the fruit of the dead, and if I wish to speak with you further I will accept the binding offer.

That is but a private wish unspoken to the living day that owns me… and even more so a mere fever dream that is destined to remain unfulfilled. Still I wonder if thoughts of me escaped with you, as I fancy some intercourse with your graduation to higher planes of existence. How arrogant of me to think that your residual self would take interest in the summaries of our correspondence, or even my interpretations of your beauty. Surely you have your own ends to relish, your own circles to tread… perhaps even debts to pay or moments to relive; it is disheartening to remind myself that our lives touched only briefly, and not with truly amorous intentions.

But save for me a seat on your otherworldly council, and I will hurry to exhaust my worldly ties and revive our playful piquet of clever words unclear. In time I shall accompany you on your pilgrimage through the valley of death… whether or not you approve of this collusion is a gamble I wish to take. Forgive me for seeking out your grave as a stranger without invitation, and forgive me for positioning our worlds in hopes that they'll collide.

Favor the Strong

I carry the weight of my heart like a child
This season of sadness is duly prolonged
Natural selection; love favors the strong
    Some die lonely but love lives on

Sands are smoothed on the backs of the mild
Time doth bury when time trudges on
Sad men will perish where sad men belong
    Some die lonely but love lives on

A martyr influx on my grave to be piled
All willingly pinned under misery's prong
For some, night is suited; for others, the dawn
    Some die lonely but love lives on

In step with their travels, I weep in the wild
I wallow in pity to make the night long
When cometh the morning, the sad will be gone
    Some die lonely but love lives on

Beware the crestfallen, so sullenly styled
Too stubborn to cross over boundaries drawn
Bitter, the man to be willfully wrong
    Some die lonely but love lives on

The prophet ignored; by the devil beguiled
My long-winded pipe knows only one song
True love is biased; love favors the strong
    Some die lonely but love lives on

Seldom

Life can be boring and beautiful at the same time; despite my better intentions, it seems I live for the dull ache that floods my heart during the comatose days of summer. I bury myself in the reserved practices of a man overlooked by youth, seeing life as but a breeze that briefly flirts with my face... yet I breathe the pockets of thought that prove influential even as they grow stale; rare retrievals of the inklings often lost in the abysmal silence of a long morning drive.

I've wasted so many warm nights at the mercy of the city's nocturnal pull, while restrained by the firm, motherly arms of my hermitage. I sulk my story to the stars, while miles away buildings bejeweled with neon lights paint a world ineffable to my experience. This world makes love without me, makes tears without me, makes bonds without me... where the clinking of martini glasses and the ramblings of midnight jazz carry on like a lullaby in vain, accompaniment to the varied stories of sleepless sinners in repose.

I long to taxi through cerulean alleys where flickering signs stain the puddles that mirror in reply, and I dream of dancing with danger as she lures me into night club corners in a dress that glimmers like serpent scales. I want to feel the crisp morning air in motion as I lean out of a limousine window, gazing upon painterly skies from a highway bridge that sparkles with rows of headlights. I want to breathe the wind that willing insomniacs taste in mouthfuls as they shout with victorious glee, and make the glorious outside world my home... in all its dynamic shades and forms. That bridge would carry me to my quarters just as the sun severs from the horizon... only then would I surrender to the cool sheets of idleness, this time next to the warm body of a newfound love. Instead I am left to ponder alone in claustrophobic circles of innocence, only moments away from turning off my bedside lamp and drifting into torpid slumber.

There is a sad victory for the sheltered one who waits to be rescued from familiar shadows... there is hope that, at least for a moment, connects my loneliness to the life beyond the dome. Nyctophiles tire as nights of glamorous indulgence give way to rust-colored dawns... Sinful escapades simmering down to their final embers, left to yield under flaming clouds that crown a populace newly laid to bed. For the duration of the dawn, we are equals... the heathens of another bygone night having submitted to temporary stagnation, caught between the boring and the beautiful in a realm that I call home.

The Goodhill Manor

My dreams have so often mimicked the Goodhill Manor,
rearranging its ivy-caked walls and maze-like gardens
so that I may partake of its native fragrances and
explore its crevices without trespass.

As always, I find it across the river;
the river that guides many a lovers' boat...
I come to the gate that drags long tails of ivy
when opened; yet it is already ajar.

Fountains of monumental girth greet me;
mossy, granite bowls teeming with lilies
that crowd against each other...
spilling upon themselves the dark opal water
whose bare, organic scent complements the floral perfumes
in a most unusual harmony.

Dwarfish bridges arch their backs over candid ponds
that, with a second look, appear to be peopled
with dragonflies and preening swans.
A gazebo crowned with a green marble clock
patiently monitors a Sunday slumber.

At the end of dawn's cycle, the church on the hill
releases the children who come to play their games
midst the gothic statues that landmark the garden maze
near the cemetery reserved exclusively for kin where
careless footsteps sometimes spill...

The graves undertake their feet without dismay,
for notions of disrespect and blasphemy are excused
in the case of children.

From yard to den steady the nests
of spirits so calm and benevolent that
the residents may never know them;
their presence akin to pictures on the wall...
as belonging as the bees and birds of the garden
and as kind as the woman that would greet us at the door.

Such a graceful contradiction that an estate
may speak of death in a warm and innocent manner...
as though mention of the after-life were doubtless and pure.

When the butler shoos the children away
and the clouds of dream begin to thin,
I leave the Goodhill Manor to its grandfatherly laurels…
wondering what luck had left it in the care of its owners
and wondering what fortunate ghosts will become its rightful heirs.

Under Lights, Over Wine

Stray cats carol in the steam of the alley, and moonlight gleams off of the power lines with a black lickerish luster... the air has a kiss betrayed by frigid teeth, but the warmth of an upscale tavern greets its guests with an earthy orange glow. Inside is a soft-spoken scene; candles flicker on white-clothed tables, multiplied in the silvery wall mirrors and empty glasses hanging bat-form above the bar.

Dinner music swelters with cultured restraint, hot lights swimming through the saxophone as it swings and dips with a seasoned musician's zeal; his eyes are shut tight, his billowed cheeks glistening with a varnish of joyful sweat. The musicians, though eccentric misfits in their daily lives, blend smoothly with their refined audience as characters belonging in an eclectic mingle.

Provoked by the lustful rasps of the brass, a man flirts with the waitress through subtle movements of his eyes and gentle flicks of his smile; they have been conversing through an unspoken language since the night began. He accomplishes this task without neglecting his heated conversation with the comrade across the table, for his eyes are swift and his voice does not appear to divide its attention.

A business-attired man kneels and proposes to his wife to be, guiding her finger into a diamond ring as she blushes the color of her dress. A small circle of observers applauds before turning back to their tables with hushed predictions of the couple's future. On cue, the waiter brings the wine list while a caterer unveils a swan ice sculpture sweating onto bottles of champagne that protrude, necks only, from a blue moat of ice.

Their jovial words are sublimated by the sound of corks being popped, followed by the lush gurgling sound of glasses being filled... the gentle clatter of silverware being unrolled from white napkin bundles, and forks tickling china as they twirl with steaming pasta. The occasional geyser of laughter spouts from the sea of mumbling voices, as scandalous secrets and embarrassing tales are told safely under the cloak of interlacing banter.

The celebration echoes out the back door of the kitchen, in a duet with the jangle of dishes being manipulated by the servants. A cook places a saucer of milk onto the cold cobblestone porch, summoning the felines out of the shadows to drink their small share of what the tavern has to offer. As the door toggles, culinary aromas escape into the brisk night air, ascending a maze of silent verandas. The city sleeps while the tavern imbues, an oasis of orange in a blue midnight haze.

All Walks of Life

Beholden to a lovely voice, we chase alluring calls
Down long forgotten corridors and faint remembered halls
A lantern keeps our innocence still litten 'cross the page
Flick'ring at the edge of void where sleep the souls enraged

Keep the fires of life at bay while tending to the spark
Touch my outstretched fingers and I'll find you in the dark
Weaving to a psalmic tune between the lives of men,
We parry those who seek to taint our universe within

Arisen wet from neighbored nests but since have traveled far
I see that you have long passed through, yet left the door ajar
Oblivion beseeches with a solemn, sweet refrain
Knocking down the apple for the temptress that remains

Greater men have sundered down where sorrow is distilled
Leaning to the intellect of scrolls and vials filled
Knowledge of the richest grade still echoes what they spake
Debriefing new inheritors of potions left to take

So take upon your weary self the burdens of small things
So that you may ne'er trip on trailing robes of kings
In eagle's eyes you'll one day see the road that you have made
The gleaming studs of jeweled pasts, in twilight do they jade

Remember my unbodied names and I'll remember thine
Suck the fruit of youth before it sickens on the vine
We whisper 'neath our headstones where in peace we close the book
Begging of our memory that last forbidden look

London Sleeps Not Tonight

Cerulean water paints rooftops in droves
O'er the city, the breath of wood stoves
There're windows aglow with the tincture of peace
And windows left cold from lanterns deceased

A young woman stands on the corner of Main
Smoking a clove in the care of the rain
Trench-coat agleam with the luster of storm
Awaiting her errand in shadows malformed

On rain-misted streets, gray moonlight is splayed
'Yond fire-lit windows there's love being made
On a warm bearskin rug piles a lacy, black dress
Virgin skin flinches to stranger's caress

From a windowsill radio, music is playing
Over the bridge carry tethered hounds baying
The rattle of keys as they turn in a gate
Unlocking a court for a duty so late

The churchyard is guarded by statues left cold
One foot on a tomb and a vocal untold
Another in armor; an angel equipped
To ward off the gargoyles that wishing well sip

The painters are many, the palette is few
For flowers in moonlight all prove to be blue
An owl in the arbor as cleansed as the snow
As though he were perched on a shoulder for show

A lonely cathedral thrusts upward its spire
Competing with buildings to reach cosmos fire
Impaling the sky like a vertical sword
With valor the urbanites daytime-adored

Aglow on the river, a gambling boat
By neon-tint waters the amorous gloat
The murmur of laughter, and toasts of esteem
And clatter of silverware echo upstream

Along the black waters, in gold lamppost gloom
A woman with breeze-tousled hair somehow groomed,
Walking with daydream gaze fixed to the ground,
Lifts up her head to the riverboat sounds

Under her footsteps, a jovial saint
The artist long gone for it's too dark to paint
High-heel claps ricochet into the dark
As they trample unknowingly over the art

The clock tower does as it's done many times
Piercing the night with gregarious chimes
Midnight you'd think was a holiday toast
The stars being guests, and the full moon its host

A midnight as this implies little harm
For London, like Paris, has womanly charm
Even the night pressures tourists to stay
Charisma that translates so smoothly from day

In Low Light

We of the human race pretend that knowledge is our servant, though we remain ignorant to the fact that servants have a mind of their own and are capable of such things as betrayal. Despite this threatening possibility, mankind sends his scientific scouts to the edge of his known reality, each time nudging that edge a little farther. As this boundary shifts, however, perception is altered and stones are overturned to expose what is often better left hidden. Men of the dark ages found brooding spirits and witchery when they thrust a mere candle into the dark… God only knows what fears we may encounter now that the electric light has expanded our radius of vision! Merciful is the meek light from the stars and moon that it may never shine fully on the secrets of earthly night, and damn the prying eyes of Man as he strains to see what could have safely been excused as shadows or hallucinations.

Observe and Obey

The most beautiful day can hide even the most potent tragedy, and the grayest of mornings may parent orchids of inspiration that sunlight could never revive. Autumn colors boiling, a backdrop for unfolding drama of insufferable hues, throw light upon life's complications brewing in the midst of nature's beauty. The seasons bear witness to countless tragedies, and countless victories therein... and if one keeps the dust of ignorance from his eyes they, too, may bear witness to the mad glamour of conflicting emotions as they urge their meanings from the periphery.

The discerning gaze of the lonely reveals prisms hiding among the day's faintest rains, and at night satellites busying among the sapphire of the stars. Humble cycles frost the fields and clear the trees of leaves, only to dissolve the pearly dust and stock the branches once again. Between these modes of season steady the marvels of cities and small towns in distress... all the while pendulums of daily life rocking gently to the tune of humanity's disheveled chords.

There is a man in the passenger seat of an automobile hurriedly passing a cemetery... his head swims with verse as he eyes the blur of headstones, comatose breath fogging the window as he struggles to capture wisps of poetic influence and shape them in his mind. As he hastily scrawls adjectives on a notepad scrap, he thinks only briefly of early morning grievers laying flowers on the graves of their departed loves... He cares, but he does not understand.

In an old world marketplace there is a woman that dances for money and sings with scant accompaniment. She sings against the pity of violins, defending the tale of true love being found midst the city's melancholic opera. There is not a soulful symphony to paint her words and promote her spirit... only the dry clamor of tambourines and the wail of mournful strings to weigh her down. By her side a leather case stands open in the dust of the alley, its cigarette-tinged bedding peppered with a sparse layer of coins... but those coins were tossed out of pity, not a shared belief in love.

At a church in Greece, bones are washed in red wine then laid to sleep, wine-scented, in an ossuary bricked for esteemed repose. The odor is sweet as to not disturb the serenity of the more developed rooms, and joins readily to the resident perfumes so long been adored by the faithful. The kitchen smells of vinegar and roses, and the chapel smells of clean water and candles that mimic confectionery aromas. The smells here are benign and comforting, but they do not lift the faces of the hunched, hooded figures that walk solemnly through the halls.

There is a dated house that crowns a dead end street, where the road melts into an empty lot sunken with gray puddles. There are bars on the windows and chains on the gates, and the vine-crippled fences that encircle seem to detest the intrusion of any new buildings on the block. Pale but well-fed flowers prod through the gates, wielding a funereal beauty crafted by a woman rarely seen in her solemn bouts of gardening. In its venerable shroud of liberated greenery, the estate is beautiful… but it is as unwelcoming as anything of beauty may be.

In an otherwise silent Himalayan monastery, a monk sobs in contrast to the peace around him. His face is warm with tears, and his cries of gibberish echo to the chill of fountain tile and brass idols. The other monks ignore him and continue to meditate with taut faces… they are compassionate beings, but they have no pity for a man who blinds himself from the guiding light with trivial tears.

And thus the mortals danced upon sentimental coals, while you watched from the shadows like the puckish eyes of demons that are quick to scribe every pitfall. Steady your hand, withdraw your finger; refrain from rippling the pools of life's spectacle with anything more than a mere interpretation. A fool's opinion is like a stone dropped in the well… but the waters will darken again after the glistening ripples have passed. Riddles are a thing of beauty, and though the very key dangles from your neck you must leave it to dangle as but a charm… There are beautiful things on the wind, things we must not question nor dirty with our touch.

Neglecting Oblivion

Portents of men writhed in oily pools and fondled the limbs of trees; not until later in time's eve did they scrape idols from bone and stretch animal skins over ceremonial drums. At first these beings carried souls that suffered in patient shadows, their deeper aspirations eclipsed by hunger and other instinctual needs. Even when caves were painted they were painted from the depths of their stomachs... desire not for enlightenment but desire for the hunt. But hunters' knees soon kneeled to parallel the ground and sow seeds of ingenious device, laying the path for a season of mortal desires enlarged... a day when the pressures of daily survival waned and allowed men to fashion religions, philosophies, and dreams of their own.

Outstretched fingers were freed to grope for the stars; watchful eyes turned to the passing comets and flung godly names to the planets. Eclipses sent shivers down the spines of priests, spawning holidays ill-prepared to survive in the memory of budding societies. Despite the inertia that still perpetuates the cycle I share with men, I fear this may all come to be in vain. Death waits for us with intentions of its own, and although it is not the end it will surely turn our chin to a different circus of wonders. Life's codes are far too long to be broken in the window of time we have been allowed, and so far the gulfs of space have not readily submitted to our efforts of defloration.

Will the mysteries of space and time remain unsolved as we leave them behind to indulge in heavenly spaces of a more personal nature? Will we abandon the secrets of the universe in exchange for inward-looking eyes? Pupils sealed in bliss, our backs to oblivion, we might quickly assume the position of naivety if a different kind of netherworld offers us a more tempting apple. Forgive us, oh fathomless nature, for we had only moments to answer the most intricate of riddles and try to unveil your treasures entrenched. Perhaps we were never meant to stray too far beyond the atmosphere that embraced our lungs, and the entertainment of nebula-misted voids was only there to dazzle our gaze as though it were an empty pearl.

She Poses with Spiders

Black hair falls on dress of red
Kneeled down by a spider's web
One hand grasps a damp fence post
The other to her kneecap close

The grass but inches from her feet
It seems like such a brazen feat
For any other woman to…
Approach a spider in the dew

Belonging in the misty fumes
Beauty winding nature's looms
Two lovely creatures in contrast
In photo opportune to last

Banished

    I have walked as a stranger through lands of unmeasured time, weaving a path through the opiate valleys in the shadow of twisting, amorphous clouds. I have gazed through unwholesome windows and crouched under strange bridges, drifted sleepily through abandoned houses and inhaled the coming storm from atop unfathomed pinnacles. Enduring the cycle of wildly integrated seasons, I've wandered through the ruins of cities renamed by nature's ascendancy, between maddening labyrinthine hallways and trees of immemorial origin. Beyond these walls the subliminal exhale of alien thunder echoes across twilit peaks, and drops of warm rain pelt a soil that many fear to tread. Here is where ephemeral gardens grow behind curious walls and gates, in erotic courtyards at the vertices of empty cross streets. I have smelled their orchids and tasted their nectar, and heard the calls of the exotic birds that nest within their vines. Here is where my mind has thought the unthinkable, and my lips have been dried by winds that pour from distant nameless grottos.

Her Majesty to Wed

She to be anointed sits with me on mattress edge
Quivering with expectation, rebel nerves alive
She pulls her silken hair back to unveil her pallid neck
She turns, anticipating pain, with nubile pupils wide

Her lips have sponged the wine, and I taste it on her breath
Wisps of incense dance aloft and cling about her robe
Devils write my life, angels sing to me in death
I whisper of these trials as I nibble on her lobe

Priests and mothers shudder at the reason why she came
Echoes fade inside her head of warnings left ignored
A kiss begins to probe the spot that swells of chosen vein
Self-surrendered to my arms, the victim so adored

Venom guides intention as it poisons through my kiss
Hell heats my arduous breath to fill her throat and chest
Canid penetration draws the color from her lips
Unlicensed union summoned by the method I know best

Spasms of her body ripple out of sync with time
First, the agony of change, and then the chill of grace
Realization stutters as her mouth moves in mime
Inducting her into a haughty exile-loving race

Soon her eyes revive with preternaturally glowing whim
My ice-lipped queen reborn to seasons previously unknown
Awakened to utopian realms when even moonlight dims
No longer am I left to ponder life's satire alone

Hearts without Quarrel

I picture my days most fruitfully spent with a woman acquired from some foreign outing in a land of high culture; I lock with her eyes from a Venetian boat as she smiles from the concrete spires of a busied riverside walkway, lowering her camera upon realizing the advent of our initial chemistry. She is wise beyond her years, dainty in composure but brute in wit; she speaks of art both Apollonian and outlandish, outdoor cafés on overcast days and books of which I've heard but only now wish to own. Together we embark on exotic travels without the hindrance of a second thought, forever adding to our experiences and embellishing the tale of our growing affection.

A vacation home planted in white sands waits for us to grace it with our auras, probed by temperate gusts that spill through open glass doors and visit the modern sculptures from room to room. After a day of tourist indulgence, my woman enters through the foyer, lays her keys on the table and quickly thereafter transforms into a goddess evening-gowned... a form that accepts me graciously in front of a hearth's humble blessing, and accompanies me on a patient walk upstairs into the care of satin sheets. After a night of instincts aflame – arguably the product of a moon-bridled lunacy shared between beasts no longer repressed – the next day eases in with the sounds of the bay soothing the cinder of forgivable sins, an ambience signified by the sigh of palm-tree ferns being fondled by the ocean breeze.

Sated is the bed where the cool sheets contrast the warm body of my lover, our legs overlapping as we sleep in dream-tickled serenity. Clutching our pillows, faces smiling obliviously to the sun as it creeps in through the gaping bay windows, we are close though we face opposite walls to allow space for comfort... a symbolism of our bold independence that remains wild even as our relationship tightens. Our love proceeds with tantric patience, a cunning passion which brandishes the blade that is our life in each other's hands... an alliance destined for the spectrum of eternity.

Our days are filled with pigeons, fountains, buildings in the blinding sun and waters sparkling from beyond the wharf... our nights are filled with velvet pillows, champagne corks, and the curvature of glassware shimmering in light subdued. The evenings smell of wine and candle fire, the mornings smell of breakfasts sunning on the balcony. The waiting arms of Athena could not gift me a better ally in eroticism, and desire could not devote its sweat to building a better structure than that of our union. Gracious is the luck that entwined our paths, and our paths will continue to enfold its blessings. Hand in hand we fulfill a dual destiny; money never an object, travel always an option... the perfect place, the perfect girl, the perfect love.

Midnight Meanings

There is an alliance that unifies the night, likened to a shared secrecy of cults and withheld by the aloof resistance of cemeteries and their resident trees. I beckon you to forgo the solace of your bed and take my hand in lieu of ritual prayer... a hand by which you will be led into a world of clandestine assembly, koans unspoken and religions forgotten yet somehow surviving in practice. It is a realm of spiritual exploration and personal heroics, an alternative to the day that finds us only in our wildest and bravest moments of nightmare reflection.

The landscape surrenders its usual palette of colors and reveals interlaced shades of onyx, opal and sapphire... the sky is a sea of indistinguishable oils, pierced only the boldest spears of star-flame... those being scythes of primitive light having survived temporal expanses unimagined my men and measured only by the divine. Any intruder here is flagged by the frosted clouds of their breath; the fumes of a heated body rising up to the moon in an effort to betray a newcomer's position. I trust that you will be brave and resolute, even as the world of darkness recognizes your steps upon the grass.

Revelations spoken in the softest of voices creep through the sleeping battle fields of conifer and birch... cryptic messages mumble beneath the conversing beasts of night, lost between nocturnal vagrants calling to one another in the dark. Wistful echoes muddy themselves into a sedate cacophony, and we accept them with cautious ears even as we hurry down the fungal steps of a timberline graveyard and into an underworld exposed... there I will watch for silhouettes along the hills as you wet your hair under the frigid moonlit falls, only moments into a brisk spring-water bathe monitored by lupine eyes gleaming in the abyss. Bare steps exit the spring, splashing water onto black stone as we break from the shadowed archways and ascend the cobalt mesa.

The westerly savannah, an observatory seat to constellations mingling in a void smeared with meteors, offers unto a sky that splinters light like a geode freckling to a modest glow. The moon with its grimace of craters bears witness to all the quarrels and affairs of mystics as they swirl in nebula's milk... above the stage where mortal anguish swoons and holds a sword to its chest. Though daybreak threatens from afar, it will only find our bodies sleeping at last and virtually unresponsive to the change. For now, the ambient orchestra of night eases into the silence of dream, and we dream on the silence of an owl's wings. No love affair fuming midst the lights of Paris could propel my heart into greater symphony, and no muse parading in daylight could better befit my desires.

Auras in Bloom

Springtime croons, so softly said like Bible hymns to children spake
Tight-wound buds unfold to flowers, glacier fists unclench to lakes
    The exodus of winter spirits sweeps away the snowy balm
   Like Hera blowing dust of diamond from the desert of her palm

   Pan alights upon a stump, his crooked legs so quaintly crossed
    Piping swift arpeggios, as branches are by breezes flossed
Vines resume their hold on tree trunks, amber sap to fill their veins
Feral horses neck with winds, pollen sifting through their manes

   Persephone, she samples trees in company of browsing deer
     Friendly beasts will not be punished for naivety to fear
  Her teeth begin to tingle as her tongue responds to sugars keen
  For slowly saturates her mouth, the juices of a nectarine

Arachne weaves an anthem gold, her fingers dancing 'cross a harp
Like spiders plucking lambent threads that glisten as the scales of carp
Her notes seduce the ears of beasts and call them to her meeting place
Fox and fowl and speckled fawn now quickened in their springtime pace

Athena prowls the orchards where betrothing thespians play their scenes
    Cradled in her rugged dress, a bounty glistens apples green
   In ling'ring here she hopes to bring her blessings to a lovers' meet
  A goddess has no other cause to search for that which mortals eat

   Lantern hues divulge the dusk; the quickly spreading sunset yolk
   A flick of a magician's wrist; night blankets with a thieving cloak
   The evening breeze assumes a chill of not so nearly winter grade
To rustle through the dappled reeds and riverbanks where love is made

 A rising moon instills the waters guarded lone by sleeping swans
The sun submerged, now circling east with promises of warmer dawns
   Orpheus now dips his pen to carry out a dreaming will
   Another chamber of the lordly hourglass now left to fill

Travelers Beware

  I am a naïve vagabond with much to see, a peddler partaking of roadside roses; hobbling along crimson clay pathways with only moments to pay to the villages he crosses. I have parted the field grasses to come upon bread-scented cottages and Shetland ponies grazing; antique facades that profess to know only the passing of swallows and the language of rickety windmills murmuring. Who knew but a sage blessed with a profound clarity that only nights ago legends sought verification in the eyes of bewildered passersby? Who knew that the ambiguous creatures that stalk my dreams... and more frequently, my nightmares... could have poisoned the very streams of the next town? Furthermore, what ill-begotten whim provokes a man to tether his horse at a questionable tavern and enter to dull his senses with ale, allowing those wild fabrications of local legend to gain leverage over his weakening mind?

  This, I say with woe, was my error to claim... to stay long enough to indulge in a town's legends, and sleep at its inns with its strange liquors in my belly. Dream-vexed in a fitful sleep, haloed with a frigid sweat that chilled my brow beyond any threshold of comfort, I slumbered in the strangeness of a dark alien room in a dark alien village... denied for that night of any homeward hopes that might steady a reflection of familiarity. My pulse quivered and resounded into my pillow, echoing the steps of werewolves clutching stolen infants in their trek across moonlit fields... the wails of restless banshees shook the flame upon my bedside candle, a flame doomed to fail under the pressure of cacophonic winds.

  The next morning woke me with reluctance, as though it pondered over leaving me for dead. Yet sunlight pried through the cracks in the ceiling to evaporate the sweat that stained my brow, and a walk to the window revealed only those Shetland ponies grazing and field workers dirtied in clouds of hay. I ignored the creaking floorboards under my feet that reminded of the previous night's unwelcome oddities, robed myself and began to shed the hex a stay in this village had put on me. Haunting dream echoes lingered in my head as I breakfasted on a sunlit veranda, memories fading with each sip of steaming tea about my lips. Soon my feet would again feel the warm clay of those summer-sweet pathways, disappearing under the shade of oak tree overhangs and leaving those legends to sleep with the town that guarded them well.

A Rebirth of Chances

    I had a dream where I was a passenger on a dismal bus, lying down on the seat in rags of disdain and guilt... I shielded my eyes from the ceiling and sobbed in pity for myself and my acquired ticket to hell, for my life's path of jealousy, rage and contempt had finally come to collect its due. The faces of the other passengers were unrealized and oblivious to me as I sank down in the cold leather and wallowed in my darkest expectations of doom. A child, a near infant with vivid blue eyes, peered over the seat in front of mine to gaze down upon me in my hour of failure with what I thought at first was bewildered disgust... but proved to be a gaze of curiosity and awe. When my tears waned and our eyes met, his face soon broke into laughter and innocent delight... and though his mouth gave only a barely audible squeal, his eyes shot through me with an endearing wave of spirited reassurance. I soon realized that this child before me, peering over, was a messenger of gracious reprieve. That blue-eyed child... was *me*.

If You So Choose

Whisper unto priestly ears of miracles purported
And never mind the ink-begotten doctrines most distorted
Even though the minds of men have slouched into depravity
Spare the roots of fantasy from coffin-sinking gravity

Immune to legends catalogued, the stolid man of reason
He's not so quick to celebrate the pagan's love of season
His chamber floor is littered with those fairy wings befallen
His head is turned against the wind that sings his angels callin'

Teach this man to resurrect his youth no longer living
The child that waits inside him for the cue of his forgiving
Wet his eyes to see again the world that he's forgotten
End the blinding drought; remove the cynic veil he's caught in

As for you, uphold your vows to forfeit wordings crass
And join his search for hidden doors, if you so choose to pass
Enter into covenants with faith whose hue runs deep
And make your choice of promises, if you so choose to keep

Hemlock Street

Those who have ambled down Hemlock Street or its neighboring avenues have witnessed a tranquil drove of secret forces working under cloak, though their eyes only saw somnolent neighborhoods shying behind oaks and willows… and dwarf mansions built on old world money, venerable in the morning mist that has ne'er parted in years. In accompanying evenings are where thoughts clouded by sleep dangle between summer and fall; mere haloes above the heads of those who rarely venture outside of their homes, even to visit their ancestors who rest in the cemetery on the opposite curb. The blade of modernism has failed to hack far into the mesh of creeper vines and English ivy, for hints of Irish mystique and Victorian charisma seem to have imported into this secluded American settlement with ease.

Tiny, fidgeting birds accent the mailbox shrubbery and brick-bordered gardens, their enchanted tittering so regretfully unheard through drowsy windows sealed and shuttered. Basket-weave rocking chairs and antique swings stagnate on the porches of flaking paint and tattered screens, hiding behind yards dominated by ancestral oak trees. One yard, though drenched in shade, flames with the pigments of a saucer magnolia in full offering; plump albino blooms half-blushing with a rosaceous tint ignited by the soil's royal nourishment. The blur of a hummingbird in plumage of multi-faceted green samples the floral chalices of nectar, too quick to be pinned by eyes slowed from a suburban evening spell. Even a trellis alive with dew-salted roses cannot wake the spectator beyond a certain degree, for the scheme of vivid flowers against pale siding and jaded wood sustains a certain chromatic balance.

Lions of stone frame the half-pried gates to the Hemlock Street Cemetery, silent sentinels each raising a paw in their frozen state of ferocity. Intruders be those who're instilled with living breath; those still carrying the pulsating heart that denies them accordance with the necrotic elite. The lots within are citied with rows of lichen-freckled tombstones, some of them applaudingly grandiose and some of them barely rising to level with the others. The curious find mossy steps beckoning to terraces of fog and willow tears… and dampened angel statues half-dipped in subtle moss tint, their melodramatic forms either caressing granite crosses or perched atop headstones in guardian pose. Under drooping tufts of peat moss sleep concrete plateaus littered with disheveled petals… the crimson contrast of scattered berries clouds the lettering on an ashy epitaph embedded in the earth.

What crouches over dark waters but a rickety bridge that protests to the weight of drifting automobiles; unbelonging vessels that carry both the mournful and the naïve to either destinations of grievance or apexes of photographic opportunity. The reflections of dense, overhanging branches ooze through the shining, streamlined bodies and speckle the ebony windows too dark to reveal the gazers within. A break in the trees beckons to a lonely hill crowned with a Civil War mausoleum; in its shadow a tiny American flag juts out of the knoll, limping in the absence of wind, and cannonball accents frame the five-step staircase that lifts up to meet the terrace.

Soon the onset of autumn expands familiar earth-tones into multiple shades of subtle variation; thousands of hues huddled within the same motif, seducing the eye with subdued yet plentiful detail. It is a smooth transition into an even sleepier era, when the mundane hardly-a-song of the crows echoes across damp, jaded fields and the rivets of woodpecker craft ricochet lonesomely through the halls of forest. Soon the cold rains will sweep the horizon and come to replenish the mist of bush-laden streets, tapping loose those residual leaves and moistening the soil of graves with a fusion fit to feed the earthen gods who demand the flow of seasons.

The Greatest of Powers

One might kneel in practice, still unwilling to obey
But he will not soon disarm the elements in play

Madmen sail, betrothed to sea
Torrid lovers needn't be
The farmer cursed with blessings naught
His fields so cancerous with drought

The ailment-ridden farmer mutters curses at the plow
The long forgotten sailor mourns the fever on his brow

Powers hurry down the list
Distribute their persuasive kiss
To pull the recluse from his lair
And cut his will by breadth of hair

To mineralize the sentimental facets of this world
Children's laughter, crystal… and elder tears, of pearl

A fragile woman in my keep
Enamored with a purpose deep
Blasphemies on walls did coat
Sonnets that the vandals wrote

Time abandons relics over which cold granite paves
Emulates the travesty of him to dance on graves

Polaris, do shine thy light
To lead the path of neophytes
Forward without doubtful thought
These powers you must question not

On His Watch

Nature, my enigmatic lover, she speaks to me through nebulous signals... a rustle of leaves, the hymns of a bird... and she cares not whether I translate them aptly. Our eccentric love affair carries on in the shadow of a higher paternal power, our spirits wed to the tune of thunder's scripture and the approval of a noble deity. Vows are spoken in riddle and the kiss is but a taste of vernal winds, but the kingdom that is revealed to me more than suffices for the lack of clarity my human form has weaned upon so childishly. Secured by an impermeable trinity, I walk through our limitless world of beauty that speaks most cordially to the unaided eye.

Glinting rays of sunlight pierce through the canopy to color the hot breath of humid forests; leaves reeking of dew drip faux honey onto the fungal nether regions of a twilit woodland. Floral scents waft through the reeds, pooling with the musk of distant rains that threaten to advance across the fields... altogether a sensual reminder of distant heavens briefly sampled in the wake of a former life. The triumphant victory cries of shell-horns echo to the music of gorges and gulleys, while the hulls of great ships crawl onto welcoming shores.

Japanese gardens boast the plumage of wild birds and roseate trees, where the flowers smell of sweetened water and their petals perpetually fall upon rain-painted cobble. Apes lounge about the ornamental steps and decorative pools, picking at seeds and splashing at Koi while their fiery manes glisten in the Eastern sun. Steaming oceans collide with cliffs and fling their spray into prisms about the air, a symphony of seabird screams accenting the drone of sifting waves. Strange, deep-dwelling beasts that feed on the carcasses of whales scour the depths in the presence of living lanterns that foster their own lunar glow.

Bat clouds bursting from a sunset cave... big, dusky moths on an old barn door... even the creatures of night receive our utmost blessing, for if nature has looked past my sins then she must look past their noir quintessence just the same. In that same vein, I am grateful to receive her father's blessing, and upon induction into the royal family I continue to explore their erudite language... the bird whose call reminds me of heaven, and the thunder whose baritone breaths awaken the most profound of distant memories.

I Am in Awe

Unfolding to the frigid morn'
A goddess unto new worlds born
Her purpose cannot be explained
Her beauty cannot be contained

Like golden silk of sunlight kin
Radiates her golden skin
Ocean water paints it wet
Varnished with a subtle sweat

Her eyes are voiced with words unspoken
Intertwining hues unbroken
Light reveals miasmal blue
And green I wish to dive into

Moving like a serpent shiver
Her touch can make a specter quiver
Yet she comes from angel dreams
And brings the warmth of evergreens

Her lips are coated with a potion
Best exampled when in motion
Hair to brush back from her eyes
Shades an ample, sultry guise

She leaves my grasp in fragrant wisps
And leaves me but a spectral kiss
The closest that she'll come to facing…
Ownership of arms embracing

Heaven's Circuit

Nature is as merciful as it is cruel; its mercy is merely concealed to the untrained eye, at least until the opportune moment. The cruelty of irony is often soothed by the aesthetics of justice via a last minute twist of fate. My twist of fate waits for me in some faint corner of existence, bathing in an odd quality of light at the end of some lone dirt path. Here memories wait for me as polished as the day they were born, as though they had never seen the future's wrath. Even my darkest nocturnal ponderings are often lit by yesterday's sun, and the legacies of far-traveled spirits return to me visions of long forgotten miracles.

There are reminiscent rooms incubated by the summer sun, complete with blowing curtains flowing in the linen-scented circulation. The carpet is warm like a father's chest, and the air is crisp like the smell of a freshly mowed lawn. Then there are dusty country roads that travel nowhere but backwards, leading to seemingly lifeless houses and shy, secluded ponds with useless boats at their dock... Things are not what they seem, but secrets are benign and nourishing to the intruder.

An eternal cycle of fragrant sunsets forever piques my imagination, as daydreams of deeper things pull me into the blushing clouds. A dragonfly's dusk hums with winged silhouettes, the cherubs of a tranquil era preceding mankind. Time is no longer a threat, but a guardian that shows me things only ones bound by my love can see. Here I will rebuild myself in the shadow of the most merciful goddess creation has ever known, my soul another child at her feet.

The world breathes with me in unison... I am at one with nature; I am at peace with even the most restless of ghosts. I no longer obsess with answers; I am content with just being another one of Earth's riddles. Heaven has more faces than I could ever imagine, and each face welcomes me like a brother rediscovered. It is time to forget trying to gain leverage over a deity and tend to matters that have been ignored for far too long... the finding of one's true inner meaning among the lucid fringes of personal conquest. He who can perceive heaven, may be able to achieve it, and with that in mind I repaint my path with hope.

'Tis a Journey

Pull up a stool or sit on a stone, my friend, there is much that we can share in the spectrum of words. I'm not unlike you; another inquisitive mortal... dazzled by beauty, groping for substance... perhaps you can find a likeness of yourself in the tales I have to tell. I bring you advice but I am no prophet, I bring you conjecture but I am no oracle. I am merely an idled bard, mobile only in the realms of the mind. A clock in my world is merely for show; time is not my chosen god. My beliefs are liquid, but my creed is inflexible... Love is a privilege, and I earn just enough to get by.

Modern pride thrives on a battle of verbal intelligence, but in the end we're all just playing with words. I am just another player in this game of letters, another voice in this strident language of pseudo-harmonious devices. Like you, I argue my case to a crowd of distracted strangers who rarely see the implications of my existence. I am of no use to them except as a sponge for scorn and ridicule, but such criticism only drives me to evolve a thicker shell to guard my thoughts.

God gave me an opponent to make me strong, and a companion to make me soft again. You, too, will find adversity within your daily travels... and I hope that you find time to carve out an ally as well. Savor every seed of benevolence you can find, and strive to equal the companion you seek so that your hands know only good works and you seldom raise a fist to the sky. Hate is the currency of a chaotic world, and there are many who awaken each day with the intention of keeping it in circulation.

I wish you great fortune, my friend, and may you never have to know the sweetness of revenge. May your journey be long, and may it linger after death. May your loves be solid and not false, and may your private haunts last long against the intentions of change. Let the tarot whisper its wisdom but not rule your world, trust not every omen that offers its influence... destiny is only suggested, not calcified, its dim outlines bending to the will of the open-minded. Always remember that all masters were once followers, and that all devils were once angels. Sometimes silence has the most enduring things to tell you, and diversity is a supplement to sanity. Messiahs come a dime a dozen, but friends are scarce... thoughts are divine, and home is an atmosphere, not a place. Religion is blind, death is transition, science is magic and trust works both ways... return to your home, never leave love and forget not these words as you tally your days.

Words, Merely Words

The poet has a greater task, when the courtship plight is through
  Soon my quill will lose its power; pretty sayings fade in hue

  Will my words be quite enough; must I also thrill to live?
Will she leave me when she finds that words are all I have to give?

EL PANDON
PETIT

Brandon Peter

CPSIA information can be obtained at www.ICGtesting.com
Printed in the USA
BVOW040011051211
277565BV00001B/44/P